Secularism's Last Sigh?
Hindutva and the (Mis)Rule of Law

Secularism's Last Sigh?
Hindutva and the (Mis)Rule of Law

BRENDA COSSMAN
RATNA KAPUR

OXFORD
UNIVERSITY PRESS

OXFORD
UNIVERSITY PRESS

YMCA Library Building, Jai Singh Road, New Delhi 110001

Oxford University Press is a department of the University of Oxford. It furthers the
University's objective of excellence in research, scholarship, and education
by publishing worldwide in

Oxford New York
Athens Auckland Bangkok Bogota Buenos Aires Calcutta
Cape Town Chennai Dar es Salaam Delhi Florence Hong Kong Istanbul
Karachi Kuala Lumpur Madrid Melbourne Mexico City Mumbai
Nairobi Paris Sao Paolo Singapore Taipei Tokyo Toronto Warsaw

with associated companies in

Berlin Ibadan

ISBN 0 19 564 813 7

Printed in India at Pauls Press, New Delhi 110 020
and published by Manzar Khan, Oxford University Press
YMCA Library Building, Jai Singh Road, New Delhi 110 001

For Kibber

Acknowledgements

We would like to thank the Law Offices of R. K. P. Shankardass, as well as the Centre for Feminist Legal Research, New Delhi, for their technical assistance and support. Thanks also to Chantal Morton and Cherie Robertson for their invaluable research assistance. We would also like to thank A. N. D. Haksar and Kanchana Natarajan for their assistance with Sanskrit translation. The authors alone, however, are responsible for the views expressed.

Contents

Preface

The mosque at Ayodhya was destroyed. Alphabet-soupists, 'fanatics', or, alternatively, 'devout liberators of the sacred site' (delete according to taste) swarmed over the seventeenth-century Babri Masjid and tore it apart with their bare hands, with their teeth, with the elemental power of what Sir V. Naipaul has approvingly called their 'awakening of history'. The police, as the press photographs showed, stood by and watched the forces of history do their history-obliterating work. Saffron flags were raised. There was much chanting of *dhuns*: *Raghupati Raghava Raja Ram & c*. It was one of those moments best described as irreconcilable: both joyful and tragic, both authentic and spurious, both natural and manipulated. It opened doors and shut them. It was an end and a beginning.[*]

Salman Rushdie

On 6 December, 1992, the 'alphabet-soupists' of Rushdie's novel, *The Moor's Last Sigh*, the RSS, BJP, and VHP combine, impaled the cause of secularism on the *trishul* of Hindutva ideology. With their 'bare hands and

[*] Salman Rushdie, *The Moor's Last Sigh*, Jonathan Cape (1995), p. 363.

teeth' they annihilated the five hundred years of bricks and mortar that held together a simple mosque—the Babri Masjid. Within minutes, the mobs of the Hindu Right had left the ancient structure in ruins, the remaining rubble occasionally belching clouds of smoke and dust, as if gasping for the last breath of secularism. The mosque lay belly up, harpooned with saffron flags and swarmed by the apostles of the God Squad ebullient in their victory over tolerance, faith and the secular ideal.

The story of the rise to power of the Hindu Right, and their struggle to determine the meaning of secularism in contemporary India corresponds to the fictional story told by Rushdie in *The Moor's Last Sigh*. His book tells the tale of the fortunes of the Da Gama-Zogoiby dynasty of Cochin, the secrets and greed that leave it divided, symbolizing the fragmentation and division that has left contemporary India divided since the emergence of the Hindu Right. The story of the family and its times is laid bare through a series of paintings known as 'The Moor Paintings'. The paintings parallel the family fortunes and the contemporary political upheavals of India, and culminate in the unsigned masterpiece, 'The Moor's Last Sigh'.

The painter, Aurora Da Gama, a 'Christian heiress', at fifteen marries Abraham Zogoiby, a 'Jewish employee', twenty-one years older than her. But India turns against them. 'Aurora da Gama and her Jew were...flies upon the great diamond of India; how dare they so shamelessly challenge the natural order of things?'[1] And the curse of Aurora's grandmother, that 'a house divided against itself cannot stand...may your house be for ever partitioned, may its foundations turn to dust, may your children rise up against you and may your fall be hard...' comes true.[2]

[1] Ibid., p. 98.
[2] Ibid., p. 99.

Moares (alias Moor) Zogoiby, their only son, 'a jewholic-anonymous, a cathjew nut, a stewpot, a mongrel cur...Yessir: a real Bombay mix'[3], is the narrator of this tale. Moor is born with a deformed right hand and ages at twice the normal speed of time. Moor is set up by his lover, Uma, (the nickname of 'Moskova'), to betray his mother, Aurora, (nicknamed 'Amrika'), a filial relationship that borders on Oedipal. He is subsequently banished from the family, devastated and alone. Uma dies and Moor is implicated in her death. He is saved from a life of rotting in jail by Raman Fielding, the Frog King, a cartoonist and religious nationalist, bearing a close resemblance to Bal Thackeray, chief of the Shiv Sena. In return for his freedom, Moor becomes one of Fielding's henchmen, using his deformity to hammer and maim Fielding's political enemies, and traitors. Meanwhile, Aurora falls to her death during one of her dance performances. '...[S]he danced without a care for the danger of it, without a downward glance towards the barnacled, patient boulders gnashing below her like black teeth.'[4] Her death, it turns out, was no accident. Moor murders Fielding in the mistaken belief that Fielding—possibly a spurned lover?—was responsible for Aurora's death. And Abraham slips into the world of organized crime, drug smuggling, prostitution—'Garam Masala, Super Quality', 'Extra Hot Chilli Peppers: Green'—and corruption. In the end, Moor learns the true identity of Aurora's killer through one of her paintings—Abraham, his father.

The story of the family represented through the paintings is interwoven with the tale of the struggle and subsequent expulsion of Boabdil from Granada and the glory and fall of the Alhambra. The early series represent a vision of hybridity and pluralism.

---

[3] Ibid., p. 104.
[4] Ibid., p. 125.

There was no stopping her. Around and about the figure of the Moor in his hybrid fortress she wove her vision, which in fact was a vision of weaving, or more accurately interweaving. In a way these were polemical pictures, in a way they were an attempt to create a romantic myth of the plural, hybrid nation; she was using Arab Spain to re-imagine India, and this land-sea-scape in which the land could be fluid and the sea stone-dry was her metaphor—idealised? sentimental? probably—of the present, and the future that she hoped would evolve. So, yes, there was a didacticism here, but what with the vivid surrealism of her images and the kingfisher brilliance of her colouring and the dynamic acceleration of her brush, it was easy not to feel preached at, to revel in the carnival without listening to the barker, to dance to the music without caring for the message in the song.[5]

But the later paintings are described as the 'dark Moors' and reflect most explicitly the subject of expulsion, referring simultaneously to the expulsion of Boabdil from Granada and the fall of the Alhambra and the banishment by the painter, Aurora, of her only son and narrator of the tale, Moor Zogoiby. The expulsion of Moor reflects the expulsion or annihilation of the minorities and the destruction of the notion of pluralism.

And the Moor-figure: alone now, motherless, he sank into immorality, and was shown as a creature of shadows, degraded in tableaux of debauchery and crime. He appeared to lose, in these last pictures, his previous metaphorical role as a unifier of opposites, a standard-bearer of pluralism, ceasing to stand as a symbol—however approximate—of the new nation, and being transformed, instead, into a semi-allegorical figure of decay. Aurora had apparently decided that the ideas of impurity, cultural admixture and mélange which had been, for most of her creative life, the closest things she had found to a notion of the Good, were in fact capable of distortion, and contained a potential for darkness as well as for light. This 'black Moor' was a new imagining of the idea of the hybrid—a Baudelairean flower, it would not be too far fetched to suggest, of evil...[6]

[5] Ibid., p. 227.
[6] Ibid., p. 303.

The moment of disillusionment reflected through Aurora's masterpiece becomes the moment of disillusionment of the Muslim minorities and all those who never questioned the country's commitment to the cause of secularism. As the mosque crumbled, the nation awakened to the fragility of secularism. In real life, the Supreme Court lamented:

Within a short time, the entire structure was razed to the ground. Indeed, it was an act of 'national shame'. What was demolished was not merely an ancient structure; but the faith of the minorities in the sense of justice and fair play of the majority. It shook their faith in the rule of law and constitutional processes. A five hundred year old structure which was defenseless and whose safety was a sacred trust in the hands of the State Government was demolished.[7]

Surely such fine words would suggest that someone in high places is committed, really committed, to upholding the principles of secularism, to holding back the tides of intolerance and Hindu majoritarianism. But, as we argue in this essay, the Supreme Court's record is not what it should be, and its performance in promoting tolerance and a respect for the rights of religious minorities less than stellar. It has certainly had its moments—in the *Bommai* decision (upholding the declaration of Presidential Rule in four states following the destruction of the mosque and the ensuing communal riots), the Court stoically and unanimously upheld the principles of secularism. But this high water mark has since been eroded. In the *Ayodhya* case (upholding the constitutionality of the Acquisition of Certain Area at Ayodhya Act 1993), the majority of the Court rejected arguments that the Act in any way violated the constitutional principle of secularism. In the name of secularism, Justice J. S. Verma praised the principle of religious toleration found in Hindu scriptures while concluding that 'a mosque is

[7] *M. Ismail Faruqui v. Union of India*, 1994 AIR SCW 4897, para 7.

not an essential part of the practice of the religion of Islam and Namaz (prayer) by Muslims can be offered anywhere, even in open' (and therefore, there was nothing to stop the State from acquiring it). In the Hindutva cases (dealing with alleged violations of the Representation of the People Act in the election speeches of the Shiv Sena and BJP) Justice Verma, again writing for the Court, not only failed to recognize the profound threat that the Hindu Right presents to Indian secularism, but actually endorsed their vision of Hindutva as secular.

This essay explores the contest over the meaning of Hindutva and secularism in the legal arena. We focus on the landmark *Hindutva* cases that represent a victory for the Hindu Right and its distinct vision of secularism. Through our discussion, what emerges is a tale about Indian secularism that is as mythical as that of *The Moor's Last Sigh*, enacted on the legal stage. The legal arena emerges as a theatrical space, where performances are constantly enacted; where there are hits and flops; where actors (the lawyers), and directors (the judges), create and recreate society and the norms by which it is governed. The content of norms and values are imbued with the passion and at times, the politics of the performers. In the re-enactment of the Ayodhya incident through the script of legal argument, we hear the cry of oppression of the Hindu majority by the Muslim minority. It underlies the justifications for the destruction of the mosque, the fabrications of the birth place of Ram being violated by the all too tangible five hundred year old structure, and the right of the Hindu masses to worship at the spot marked with an 'x'. The identity of the Hindus is re-formulated and re-imagined through the ideology of Hindutva, as a monotheistic religion, located in the *shilyanya* bricks that would be used to build the temple, the undisputed home of the solo-Hindu deity—Ram. The arguments justifying the destruction of the mosque were premised on the concept of secularism and toleration based on religious identity. In this instance, the Muslims were accused of demonstrating their intolerance by eradicating the *janambhoomi* (birth place) of Hindu belief and religious practice.

The Hindu Right's accelerated rise to power at the close of the twentieth century becomes a historical conundrum that can neither be ignored nor toppled at a moment's notice. Enthroned as the ruling party in the March 1998 national elections, the Bharatiya Janata Party (BJP) installed Atal Bihari Vajpayee as the Prime Minister. The BJP represents the force of the Hindu Right that must be met and challenged at the level of ideology, at the level of the discursive struggle over the content and meaning of secularism. The Hindu Right is currently heady with power, attempting to present itself as omnipotent, even as it clings to a razor's edge in Parliament. As Arundhati Roy recently stated, 'Governments change. They wear masks within masks. They moult and re-invent themselves all the time. The one we have at the moment, for instance, does not even have enough seats to last a full term in office, but demands that we trust it to do pirouettes and party tricks with nuclear bombs even as it scrabbles around for a foothold to maintain a simple majority in Parliament.'[8]

Yet the BJP continues to pursue its agenda undeterred. Indeed deterrence, nuclear deterrence, has become the mantra of the moment, seeking the avoidance of nuclear war through the construction of bombs of mass destruction. Deterrence through mutual obliteration: now there's an almighty contradiction. The Hindu Right aims to establish Hinduism as supreme, as the mother of all religions, gods, faiths, and creeds. But the party's first major act while in power has been to conduct nuclear tests in the heart of Rajasthan, to clear the way for the birth of the

[8] Arundhati Roy, 'The End of Imagination', *Outlook*, August 3, 1998 p. 64.

'mother of all bombs', which if used, will in Arundhati Roy's words, prove to be the greatest equalizer. There is a perversity in this contradiction that advocates the supremacy of Hinduism armed with a nuclear warhead. And it was in revolt against such perversities, which know no limits, that Aurora danced her 'profane gyrations' until she herself became the very receptacle of the perversity she challenged.

Hindutva and the bomb constitute a lethal arsenal unleashed by the Right to promote its peculiar doctrine of secularism and tolerance. Yet why were we surprised? It was there in the BJP Election Manifesto all along. In fact, an awful lot has always been there in their manifestos, speeches, and party newspapers. One can hardly accuse them of mincing their words. While they speak with different voices, there is always at least one voice quite willing to admit how much they hate minorities, and outline the threat that they supposedly present to the very fabric of the nation.

In this essay, we look at the political rhetoric of Hindutva. In particular, we examine its use of liberal rights discourse as a means for delivering its messages of hate and destruction. The visible exponents of this message are Atal Bihari Vajpayee and his counterpart, L. K. Advani, the Home Minister. This duo ostensibly constitute the more moderate voice of the Right wing. We propose several strategies for engaging with the Right at both an ideological and strategic level. The Right is not a homogenous, monolithic entity. Beneath the translucent glass skin of unity and consensus are cracks and fissures. Picking away the shards of broken skin is a potent and essential strategy for progressives and others seeking to reveal the fragmentation and divisiveness that lies beneath the surface façade. We also suggest ways in which the discourse of secularism as deployed by the Right in law, can and should be countered through a notion of toleration based on a political principle of respect. Respect is a concept that remains elusive to the Right, as much as tolerance has become mangled in their conception of a better world, where Hindus will reign supreme and the trammelled body of secularism will be reconstructed and recast in the image of Hindu cultural nationalism and ethnic purity.

This essay was originally written at a time somewhere in between the most inauspicious of events: after the destruction of the Babri Masjid, and before the detonation of the nuclear bombs at Pokhran: after the Hindu Right had come to power in Maharashtra, and before its ascendence to power at the Centre. Those of us who condemned the antics of the Hindu Right at the time were told by many that we were being overdramatic, a little too conspiratorial, a little sensationalistic, that we just took them too seriously. We are not sure what would change the minds of those who do not see the slow infiltration of the Hindu Right not just into power, but into the hearts and minds of average people—average Hindu people at least. Surely, the idea that Right wing ideologues now have their finger on the button, that they hold not only political power but the power of nuclear holocaust should be enough to take them seriously. 'But that's a different issue', the recalcitrant secularist tells us, 'of course one is against the bomb, but that has nothing to do with the role of the courts'. Well, it may be a step or two away, but the Hindu Right's version of cultural nationalism has no problem making these connections. Their vision of Hindutva is being pursued on many fronts—from judicial to nuclear. We are not suggesting that these are the same—there is quite a difference between a bad judgement and a nuclear bomb (and we would much rather endure the former to the latter). But, we are suggesting that the ideology underlying both their judicial and nuclear incursions is the same. It is an ugly blend of hatred and intolerance, and wildly inflated infallibility. Our work is a small attempt at challenging that ugliness, at just one of its many sites. It is a small attempt to reveal the incursions that the Hindu Right has made into the legal arena.

On the rewriting of this essay—after the BJP's rise to political power, Pokhran II, and the unrelenting insistence by the VHP that the temple *will* be built—we rightly stand accused of taking them very seriously indeed.

Introduction

India forces us to think, sometimes in tragic moments, of the function of religious thought within secularism. This is again a challenge for the times. If you look around the world today this is a very important issue; this particular kind of sometimes fundamentalist, of other times religious orthodoxy erupting within secularism, not simply in opposition to it.

*Homi Bhabha**

Secularism has never been taken for granted in India. The struggle to secure its constitutional and political protection has been long and hard, and its enemies continue to be multiple. But recently, as Homi Bhabha has suggested, the enemies of secularism are waging their war not in opposition to secularism, but in and through it. Increasingly, secularism has become the site of intensive political contestation, in which right wing, religious and fundamentalist forces endeavour to claim the terrain as their own. In India, the Hindu Right—a

* Interview with Homi Bhabha, 19:12 *The Book Review*, Dec 1995.

nationalist and right wing political movement devoted to creating a Hindu State—has increasingly staked out its own claim to secularism, arguing that it alone is committed to upholding this constitutional principle. Indeed, secularism has become a central and powerful weapon in the Hindu Right's quest for discursive and political power.[1] These struggles over the meaning of secularism, and the place of religion in politics, have entered the legal arena. The courts have been called upon to adjudicate the claims for and against secularism, and whether the strategies of the Hindu Right violate this basic constitutional principle. A series of recent, and highly controversial cases involved the prosecution of elected representatives of the Hindu nationalist Shiv Sena/Bharatiya Janata Party alliance government in the western state of Maharashtra for corrupt practices under the Representation of the People Act, 1951. In *Manohar Joshi v. Nitin Bhaurao Patil*,[2] and eleven others (collectively known as the Hindutva cases) the Supreme Court of India delivered a mixed message to the cause of secularism. On the one hand, the Court found several of the accused—most notably the Shiv Sena leader Bal Thackeray, one of the most militantly pro-Hindu, and anti-Muslim voices within the Hindu Right— guilty of both appealing to religion to gain votes, and promoting religious enmity and hatred. But the Court also held that 'Hindutva', the ideological linchpin of the Hindu Right's efforts to establish a *Hindu Rashtra* (Hindu state), simply represented

---

[1] See Ratna Kapur and Brenda Cossman, 'Communalising Gender/ Engendering Community: Women, Legal Discourse and the Saffron Agenda', in *EPW*, 35 (May 1993), p. 28; revised version reproduced in Tanika Sarkar and Urvashi Butalia (eds), *Women and The Hindu Right* (New Delhi: Kali for Women, 1995), p. 82. See generally, Ratna Kapur and Brenda Cossman, *Subversive Sites: Feminist Engagement with Law in India* (New Delhi: Sage, 1996).

[2] AIR 1996 SC 796. Also reported in 1996 (1) SCC 169.

'a way of life in the sub-continent', and was not in and of itself a violation of the Representation of the People Act, 1951. The decisions provoked both celebration and outrage. The Hindu Right has heralded the decision as ushering in a new era of Hindutva, while the democratic secular forces committed to fighting the communalization of political and social life by the Hindu Right have routinely denounced the decision.[3]

In this essay, we examine two deeply problematic aspects of the Supreme Court's judgment. First, we argue that the Supreme Court erred in concluding that Hindutva constitutes a 'way of life' of the people of the subcontinent, and that its deployment constitutes neither a violation of the prohibition on appeal to religion to gain votes nor a violation of the prohibition on promoting religious enmity and hatred. We argue that the Supreme Court erred in eliding its discussion of the meaning of Hinduism with the meaning of Hindutva, and that its conclusions on Hindutva are without legal precedent or authority. Moreover, by examining the historical and political context within which the concept of Hindutva has acquired meaning, we argue that Hindutva cannot be separated from its appeal to religion, nor from its assault on the legitimacy of religious minorities.

Secondly, we argue that the Supreme Court erred in its acceptance of the secular nature of the speeches of the Hindu Right. By examining the broader discursive struggles over the meaning of secularism in India, we illustrate the extent to which the Supreme Court's conclusion has effectively vindicated the profoundly anti-secular vision of secularism that the Hindu Right has long been trying to promote. In so doing, we challenge

[3] A writ petition seeking a review of one of the decisions, *Manohar Joshi*, was dismissed by the Court, reaffirming the decision of the Court in these cases. See *Mohd. Aslam v. Union of India*, AIR 1996 SC 1611.

the Supreme Court's views that there is nothing inconsistent between its conclusions in the Hindutva cases and its earlier decisions. We further argue that the conclusion in the Hindutva cases, and the significant victory it represents for the Hindu Right, has been facilitated by the failure to take these discursive strategies of the Hindu Right seriously and pay sufficient attention to the specific manipulations of secularism occurring at its hands. As we have argued elsewhere, the Hindu Right has hijacked the dominant understanding of secularism as the equal respect for all religions to promote its vision of Hindutva, and its agenda of establishing a Hindu State.[4] In its hands, the concept of equal respect for all religions becomes a tool for attacking the rights of minority religious communities. Its emphasis on formal equality—that is, on the formal equal treatment of all religions—operates as an unmodified majoritarianism whereby the majority Hindu community becomes the norm against which all others are to be judged and treated. After reviewing this discursive strategy, we argue that in failing to pay sufficient attention to these strategies, and particularly, in failing to more clearly articulate an alternative vision of equality that must inform the concept of equal respect for all religions, the forces of democratic secularism including the Supreme Court have left the door ajar, and unwittingly allowed the Hindu Right to continue their discursive strategy of hijacking secularism for their own very unsecular agenda.

In the final section, we turn to consider the crisis of secularism in India, and attempt to suggest ways of engaging with contemporary secular discourses. After briefly reviewing some of the debates on secularism's future (or its lack thereof), we suggest a discursive strategy for reappropriating the dominant discourses of secularism from the Hindu Right, and

[4] See n. 1 above.

reshaping this discourse in a way that may better capture and promote a democratic political vision. Despite some of the limitations of a vision of secularism based on equal respect for all religions, we search for the interpretative possibilities for revitalizing secularism within this vision. The challenge is, we believe, one of promoting toleration where it has been increasingly eroded, and countering the majoritarianism that has swamped the ideal of equal respect for all religions. We explore each of the three core principles that have informed Indian secularism—equality, freedom of religion and toleration—and offer some tentative suggestions for revitalizing these principles to better meet the challenge of majoritarianism.

1

The Hindu Right

By 'Hindu Right', we are referring to the main organizations and political parties in the current phase of Hindu communalism[1] in India—the Bharatiya Janata Party (BJP), the Rashtriya Swayam Sevak Sangh (RSS), and the Vishwa Hindu Parishad (VHP), as well as the militantly anti-Muslim Shiv Sena—which are collectively seeking to establish a Hindu state in India. The central ideology of this political

---

[1] Communalism has been defined as a discourse based on the 'belief that because a group of people follow a particular religion, they have as a result, common social, political and economic interests'. Bipan Chandra, *Communalism In Modern India*, 1984, p. 1. It is a discourse that attempts to constitute subjects through communal attachment, particularly, through religious community. The construction of communal identities—most notably, Hindu and Muslim—has been a central characteristic of the modern Indian polity, and continues to be an important source of political fragmentation. Through communal discourse, subjects come to understand the world around them as one based on the conflict between religious groups, and Indian society is understood as fractured by the conflict between these groups. Although India is characterized by many other equally-compelling sources of division—class, caste, language, region—communalism has been, and remains amongst the most politically divisive and explosive of identities.

movement is Hindutva—literally translated as 'Hinduness'—which seeks to establish the political, cultural and religious supremacy of Hinduism, and the Hindu nation. The Hindu Right dates back to the nineteenth century revivalist and nationalist movements in India, which sought to revitalize Hindu culture as a strategy of resisting colonialism. As it developed through the twentieth century, particularly in the writings of Savarkar in the 1920s, it has taken on a distinctively right-wing, anti-minority stance. As Basu and others have stated, '[a]t the heart of Hindutva lies the myth of a continuous thousand year old struggle of Hindus against Muslims as the structuring principle of Indian history. Both communities are assumed to have been homogenous blocks—of Hindu patriots, heroically resisting invariably tyrannical, 'foreign' Muslim rulers'.[2] More recently, it is said, the policy of appeasing minorities, that is, of special treatment for Muslims and other religious minorities has perpetuated the oppression of Hindus. The contemporary social, economic and political malaise that is ostensibly gripping Hindu society is seen to lie in this policy of appeasement. The answer to the crisis, according to the discourse of the Hindu Right, lies in establishing a *Hindu Rashtra*: India must be a Hindu State.[3]

The Hindu Right has sought to promote and spread this communalized discourse to an increasingly large segment of Hindu society, particularly with the creation of the VHP in 1964. Founded at the behest of the RSS, the VHP was intended to infuse the politics of Hindutva with a specifically religious

[2] Tapan Basu et al., *Khaki Shorts, Saffron Flags: A Critique of the Hindu Right*, (1993), p. 2.

[3] This movement has been variously labelled and debated as 'Hindu fundamentalist', 'Hindu fascist',and/or 'Hindu nationalist', among others. We use the term 'Hindu Right' to demarcate both the communal and highly conservative nature of their agenda.

vision. Unlike the RSS, which functioned as an elite organization, the VHP was intended to popularize the Hindutva ideology among the masses.[4] And this phase of populism has been characterized by an increasingly extreme and violent anti-Muslim rhetoric. Although the rhetoric of the earlier leaders of the Hindu Right, notably Savarkar and Golwalkar, were certainly characterized with a strong anti-Muslim stance, the rhetoric of leaders such as Bal Thackeray (the leader of the Shiv Sena) seems to have reached new heights. For example in an interview in the *Time* magazine in the immediate aftermath of the Bombay riots in 1993,[5] Thackeray did not mince words on his agenda for the Muslim minority in India.[6] When questioned on the role of Shiv Sena in the riots, Thackeray replied: 'I want to teach Muslims a lesson'. When questioned on the fact that

[4] For a more detailed discussion, see Basu *et al*, n. 2 above.

[5] The Bombay riots broke out in the aftermath of the destruction of the mosque at Ayodhya, when communal riots swept across India. The first phase of the Bombay riots occurred immediately after the destruction of the mosque on December 6, 1992, and continued for six days. Official figures claim that 200 people died, although many independent inquiries place the figure over 400. The majority are said to have died as a result of indiscriminate police firing. The second phase of the rioting, which took place from January 5–15, 1993, were of a very different nature. These riots were a confrontation between Shiv Sainiks and Muslims, and by most accounts, were explicitly provoked by the Shiv Sena. As the city burned for ten days, the rest of the country reeled. Bombay has long been considered India's most cosmopolitan centre. Home to the financial and entertainment industries, its heterogeneous culture gave the impression that the city was less prone to the volatile nature of communal hatred and violence. As that image went up in the riot's flames, committed secularists were left with a profound sense of doubt and anxiety about the future of India's secular democracy. For a more detailed discussion, see Asghar Ali Engineer, 'Bombay Shames India' *EPW*, (Jan 16, 1993) p. 81; and Flavia Agnes, 'Two Riots and After: A Fact-finding Report on Bandar (East)' *EPW* (Feb 13, 1993) p. 265. See more generally, the Report of the Sri Krishna Commission on the Bombay Riots, released August 6, 1998.

[6] Interview with Bal Thackeray, *Time*, Jan 25, 1993, p. 43.

Muslims were fleeing Bombay in droves, Thackeray replied 'If they are going, let them go. If they are not going, *kick them out.*' In an exchange that reflects his long-standing admiration of the Hindu Right for Nazi Germany, he responded to the charge that 'Indian Muslims are beginning to feel like Jews in Nazi Germany', by saying 'Have they behaved like the Jews in Nazi Germany? If so, there is nothing wrong if they are treated as Jews were in Germany.'[7]

These are a few of the more extreme of Thackeray's invectives. But there is no scarcity of them. The *Dopahar Ka Saamna* (the mouthpiece of the Shiv Sena) is loaded with such hate-filled attacks on the Muslims. Muslims are routinely attacked as 'barbaric' and 'uncivilized'; as 'traitors who partitioned the country'; as 'traitors who should be condemned'. Time and again, Muslims are alleged to be the puppets of Pakistan, as loyal only to Pakistan, and thus, as a threat to India's national security.[8] Moreover, Thackeray is not alone in this virulently anti-Muslim rhetoric. Sadhvi Rithambhara—a leading figure with the VHP and one of the few high-profile

---

[7] Ibid.

[8] For instance, in an editorial that appeared in *Saamna* on March 12, 1996 following the defeat of Pakistan in the quarter finals of the World Cup Cricket, the fact that several skirmishes broke out between Indians who were fans of the Pakistani team, and Indians who were celebrating India's victory, was taken as evidence of the traitorous character of all Muslims. 'Why should these rioting Muslims of Malvani [a suburb of Bombay where the confrontation took place] not be chased away to Pakistan? What right do they have to live in India? Such traitors should be condemned by all countrymen... It is Muslims like those in Malvani that the Shiv Sena hates and resolves once again to chase away. This is a warning to Malvani's Muslims. They should behave themselves, rid themselves of the Pakistan disease and join the national mainstream. Otherwise they will be the target of Hindu anger this time... If now, even a single stone is thrown at any Hindu, rivers of blood will flow in Malvani. This is the resolve not only of Hindus from Malad but all over India'.

women within the Hindu Right—repeatedly lashes out against the Muslim community, for allegedly keeping Hindus in a state of persecution.[9] The general sentiment that Hindus are oppressed is often followed by increasingly violent rhetoric calling on Hindus to fight back against these Muslim oppressors, and expressly calling for violent confrontation.[10] The rhetoric of these leaders is thus not only increasingly hateful, but also increasingly advocates violence against the Muslim community. Although Muslims are a favourite target, they are not alone in suffering the wrath of the Hindu Right. The Christian community also comes under attack, as a foreign threat to the (Hindu) fabric of the nation. For example, activists from the Bajrang Dal—another extreme wing of the Hindu Right—have recently set fire to copies of the Bible on the basis of their (perpetual) fear of forced conversions.[11]

[9] In a very common statement, Sadhvi rants: 'The long suffering Hindu is being called a religious zealot today only because he wants to build the temple. The Muslims got their Pakistan. Even in a mutilated India, they have special rights. They have no use for family planning. They have their own religious schools. What do we have? An India with its arms cut off, an India where restrictions are placed on our festivals, where processions are always in danger of attack, where the expression of our opinion is prohibited, where our religious beliefs are cruelly derided.' Quoted by Sudhir Kakar 'Sudhir Kakar analyses Sadhvi Rithambhara's speech' unpublished paper.

[10] For instance, in the time leading up to the destruction of the mosque at Ayodhya, Sadhvi could be heard calling for a final fierce battle with the Muslims: 'If there has to be bloodshed, let it happen once and for all' (as quoted in Basu et al., see n. 2 above, p. 73. Several efforts have been made to bring criminal charges against Sadhvi for promoting religious enmity and hatred. To date, however, these charges have all been dismissed by the courts. For a more detailed discussion of hate speech laws and the Hindu Right, see Ratna Kapur 'Who Draws the Line? Feminist Reflections on Speech and Censorship' EPW, (April 20, 1996) WS 15–30.

[11] Times of India, July 27, 1998. The VHP has also been involved in vandalizing Christian cemeteries, as well as a range of other attacks on the

The Shiv Sena and the VHP represent some of the more extreme elements within the Hindu Right. Much of the rhetoric of the BJP is considerably more moderate, presenting a face of respectability for the purposes of electoral politics. Further, there are many internal differences and contradictions within the Hindu Right, on a range of social, economic and political issues.[12] But, despite these differences, the various elements are all united in their general political project of promoting Hindutva and establishing a Hindu state. There are a set of core beliefs that appear to unite the various players—a cultural nationalism based on Hinduism, an attempt to rewrite the nationalist narrative in and through this Hindu script, an effort to establish a nation state that embodies this nationalist narrative of Hindutva, and a common refrain: teaching the minorities a lesson. The ways in which these beliefs are articulated may take different forms, with different degrees of hostility directed towards those who are perceived to most threaten their Hindu nationalist script. For example, the Shiv Sena thinks little of its vituperative attacks on the Muslim minority, whereas the BJP's now successful quest for political power has necessitated a more accommodative rhetoric that speaks only of eliminating the 'appeasement of minorities'. Yet, both in its moderate and extremist forms, the Hindu Right is united in its targeting of

---

Christian and Muslim communities in the state of Gujarat. The National Minorities Commission is currently investigating the escalation in these extremist activities in the state. The Bajrang Dal is also the organization responsible for the repeated attacks on M. F. Hussain and his artworks.

[12] For example, in *Subversive Sites*, (see Introduction, n. 1), we noted the many contradictions within the Hindu Right in terms of its discourse and policies on gender. Rather than focusing on the more extreme or orthodox views on women, we chose to focus on the more moderate voice of the Hindu Right.

the Muslim minority as a threat to the Hindu Nation. In this essay, we deploy the term 'Hindu Right' to refer to this BJP-RSS-VHP-Shiv Sena combine—the 'alphabet soupists'—not to obscure the important differences within this movement, but rather to capture their underlying shared vision. Our focus, in particular, is on the meaning that the Hindu Right gives to the terms 'Hindutva' and 'secularism'—two terms that are central to their very political identity and around which at least a certain degree of consensus is decipherable.

Although the Hindu Right has long been a player in India's political scene, its political power has dramatically increased over the last decade. The Ayodhya campaign, in which it sought to have the Babri Masjid, a Muslim mosque dating back to the sixteenth century, replaced with a Hindu temple, proved to be enormously successful in generating broad-based support for the Hindu Right. The VHP, and subsequently, both the RSS and the BJP, stirred up a controversy of enormous proportion, alleging that the mosque was built on the site of the birth of the Hindu god Ram. The Hindu Right demanded that the Babri Masjid be removed, and that a temple commemorating the birth of Ram be built in its place. The campaign succeeded in mobilizing thousands of supporters, some of whom followed the marchers to Ayodhya, while many others sent money and bricks to help construct the new temple. After a steady escalation in the anti-Muslim political rhetoric, and the demands for the destruction of the mosque, a mob destroyed the Babri Masjid on 6th December, 1992. The destruction of the mosque triggered massive communal riots around the country, in which thousands of people were killed.

Following the destruction of the mosque, and the ensuing communal riots, the President of India dismissed the BJP governments in four states, and the central government cracked down on many of the Hindu Right organizations. But the government was unable to break the growing support for the Hindu Right. The bans on the organizations and their publications, as well as the dismissal of the state governments only seemed to strengthen the resolve of the Hindu Right, and its claim that it alone could protect real democracy and real secularism in India. While many of the political leaders of the BJP could not condone the violent destruction of the mosque, neither did they condemn the destruction. Despite the national outcry condemning the Hindu Right, and the role of the BJP in the destruction and the violence that followed in its wake, the political momentum of the BJP continued to grow. The ban on the RSS was held to be unsustainable, and although the declaration of Presidential Rule was upheld by the Supreme Court,[13] the state governments that were dismissed were ultimately re-elected.

In the 1996 national elections, the BJP, though short of a majority, emerged as the largest single political party, and was asked to form the government, and Atal Bihari Vajpayee—the party's leader—became India's Prime Minister. Since it was unable to secure the support required to form a coalition government, the BJP government fell within two weeks. Despite its rapid rise and fall as the nation's government, the enormous increase in the BJP's popularity among the Indian electorate could not be ignored. In the 1998 elections, following the collapse of the United Front government (an unstable alliance of India's regional parties and the Left, with Congress supporting the coalition from the outside), the BJP again

---

[13] *S. R. Bommai v. Union of India*, AIR 1994 SC 1918.

emerged as the largest single party, and was again asked to form the government. But this time, with 177 seats in Parliament, the BJP successfully formed a coalition with eighteen different political parties. In March 1998, the BJP-led coalition was sworn into office, with Vajpayee as the new Prime Minister of India.[14]

But the Hindu Right is not only a political party, and the political inroads of the BJP must be seen in the broader context of the struggles of the Hindu Right as a whole. The RSS-BJP-VHP combine has been engaged in a discursive struggle, in which they have attempted to establish their vision of Hindutva as ideologically dominant. Through their collective efforts, they have sought to naturalize the ideas of Hindutva, by making these ideas a part of the common sense of an increasingly large segment of Hindu society. The Hindu Right's struggle for ideological dominance has stretched across a broad range of fields from history to politics, religion to economics. Our own focus is on the struggle for meaning within the field of law, and on the ways in which the Hindu Right has sought to deploy a host of legal concepts and constitutional principles in order to advance its political agenda.[15] In particular, we focus on what we believe to be a highly significant development in the Hindu

[14] The need to form a coalition, however, forced the BJP to compromise on some of its Election Manifesto commitments. In the National Agenda for Governance, 1998, the BJP was forced to abandon part of its Hindutva platform, including any reference to the construction of the temple at Ayodhya, the amendment of Article 30 or 370 of the Constitution, and the introduction of a Uniform Civil Code. Article 30 guarantees religious minorities the right to establish and adminster their own educational institutions. Article 370 provides special status for Jammu & Kashmir.

[15] For further discussion of the way in which the Hindu Right has sought to deploy law and legal discourse in its discursive struggles, see *Subversive Sites*, (Introduction, n. 1).

Right's efforts to infuse the constitutional principles of secularism and equality with new meaning, consistent with its vision of Hindutva, namely, the recent Supreme Court of India's judgment in the Hindutva cases. We attempt to situate this judgment within the broader context of the discursive struggles of the Hindu Right and its efforts to legitimize its vision of Hindu supremacy.

2

The Supreme Court
·Hindutva Judgments

In the cases of *Manohar Joshi* and eleven others,[1] the election of Shiv Sena/BJP candidates in the December 1987 state elections in Maharashtra were challenged as having committed corrupt practices in violation of section 123 of the Representation of the People Act, 1951. Section 123(3) of the Act prohibits candidates from any appeal to his or her religion, race, caste, community or language to further his or her prospect for election, or to prejudicially affect the election of any other

[1] Introduction n. 2. The other cases were as follows: *Prabhoo v. Prabhakar Kasinath Kunte and Ors*. AIR 1996 SC 11 113, with *Shri Bal Thackeray v. Shri Prabhakar Kasinath Kunte and Ors*; *Ramachandra G. Kapse v. Haribansh Ramakbal Singh* AIR 1996 SC 817; with *Pramod Mahajan v. Haribansh Ramakbal Singh and Anr.*, and *Sadhvi Reetambrara* [sic] *v. Haribansh Ramakbal Singh and Anr.*; *Ramakant Mayekar v. Smt. Celine D'Silva* AIR 1996 SC 826; with *Chhagan Bhujbal v. Smt. Celine D'Silva and Anr., Balasaheb Thackeray v. Smt. Celine D'Silva*; *Shri Moreshwar Save v. Shri Dwarkadas Yashwantrao Pathrikar* AIR 1996 SC 3335; *Chandrakanta Goyal v. Sohan Singh Jodh Singh Kohli* AIR 1996 SC 861; *Suryakant Venkatrao Mahadik v. Saroj Sandesh Naik*, (1995) 7 Scale 92.

candidate.[2] Section 123(3A) prohibits candidates from promoting 'feelings of enmity or hatred between different classes of the citizens of India on grounds of religion, race, caste, community or language' for the purposes of gaining votes, or prejudicially affecting the votes of another candidate.[3] Charges were brought against twelve members of the Hindu Right, including Bal Thackeray, leader of the Shiv Sena and Manohar Joshi, Chief Minister of Maharashtra for violating these provisions.[4]

At the Supreme Court, the main opinion on the interpretation of the Representation of the People Act, 1951 and whether an appeal to Hindutva constituted a violation of the Act, was rendered in the case of *Prabhoo v. Prabhakar Kasinath Kunte & Others* which involved charges of corrupt practices against Dr Prabhoo, the Mayor of Bombay, and his agent Bal Thackeray.[5]

---

[2] Section 123(3) provides 'The appeal by a candidate or his agent or by any other person with the consent of a candidate or his election agent to vote or refrain from voting for any person on the ground of his religion, race, caste, community or language or the use of, or appeal to religious symbols or the use of, or appeal to, national symbols, such as the national flag or the national emblem, for the furtherance of the prospects of the election of that candidate or for prejudicially affecting the election of any candidate.'

[3] Section 123 (3A) provides, 'The promotion of, or attempt to promote, feelings of enmity or hatred between different classes of the citizens of India on grounds of religion, race, caste, community or language, by a candidate or his agent or any other person with the consent of a candidate... for the furtherance of the prospects of the election of that candidate or for prejudicially affecting the election of any candidate.'

[4] Charges were brought against twelve individuals, but several of the charges were joined into a single case, resulting in seven separate decisions.

[5] See n. 1 above. The *Manohar Joshi* case is often considered to be the main opinion, and is the decision that is most often referred to by commentators on the Hindutva cases. However, in our view, it is clearly the *Prabhoo* decision that provides the main opinion on the specific question of whether Hindutva constitutes a violation of the Representation of the People Act. On this point, the opinion in *Joshi* simply refers to the opinion in *Prabhoo*.

The Bombay High Court had found Prabhoo and Thackeray guilty of corrupt practices on the grounds that they had appealed for votes on the ground of religion, and promoted feelings of enmity and hatred between different classes of citizens of India. On appeal, Prabhoo challenged the constitutionality of section 123 of the Representation of the People Act, 1951 on the grounds that it violated the fundamental right to freedom of speech in Article 19(1) of the Constitution. It was further argued that the High Court had erred in finding that an appeal to 'Hindutva' constituted a violation of the Act. It was argued that Hindutva means Indian culture, not Hindu culture, and moreover, that the public speeches of the candidate 'criticized the anti-secular stance of the Congress Party in practising discrimination against Hindus and giving undue favour to the minorities which is not an appeal for votes on the ground of Hindu religion.'[6]

The Supreme Court first turned to the question of the meaning of section 123(3), that is, the prohibition of appeals to religion to gain votes. In the Court's view, the prohibition did not mean that religion could never be mentioned in election speeches. A speech 'with a secular stance' which raised questions about discrimination against a particular religion would not be caught by section 123(3). Rather, section 123(3) was intended to prohibit a candidate from seeking votes on the basis of his religion, or from trying to capture votes from another candidate on the basis of that candidate's religion. The Court then considered the question of the meaning of the prohibition on the promotion of feelings of enmity or hatred between different religious communities contained in section 123(3A). In its view, the clear objective of the section was to curb 'the tendency to promote or attempt to promote communal, linguistic or any

[6] Ibid., p. 1119, para 7.

other factional enmity or hatred to prevent the divisive tendencies'.[7] The Court accepted the arguments of the appellants that the prejudicial effect on public order is implicit in this section.[8]

The Court subsequently considered and rejected the constitutional challenge to sections 123(3) and 123(3A)[9], and then turned to consider the meaning of Hindutva and Hinduism, and whether an appeal to Hindutva constitutes a violation of these

[7] Ibid., p. 1123, para 20.

[8] In considering the meaning of this section, the Court quoted at length from the earlier Supreme Court decision in *Ziyauddin Burhanuddin Bukhari v. Brijmohan Ramdass Mehra* 1975 (Suppl) SCR 281: 'It seems to us that section 123, subsections (2), (3) and (3a) [sic] were enacted so as to eliminate, from the electoral process, appeals to those divisive factors which arouse irrational passions that run counter to the basic tenets of our Constitution, and, indeed, of any civilized political and social order. Due respect for the religious beliefs and practices, race, creed, culture and language of other citizens is one of the basic postulates of our democratic system...'. ibid., p. 1124, para 22. In *Bukhari*, the Court further held: 'We have to determine the effect of statements proved to have been made by a candidate, or, on his behalf and with his consent, during his election, upon the minds and feelings of the ordinary average voters of this country in every case of alleged corrupt practice... In all such cases, the line has no doubt to be drawn with care so as not to equate possible impersonal attacks on religious bigotry and intolerance with personal ones actuated by bigotry and intolerance.'

[9] In considering whether section 123 constituted a reasonable restriction to the right to free expression which was permissible under Article 19(2) of the Constitution, the Court concluded that the provision should be upheld in the interests of 'decency or morality'. The Court was of the view that this clause was not confined to sexual morality, but included action that was against the current standards of behaviour or propriety. *Prabhoo*, (n. 1 above, p. 1126 para 29). It held that 'In a secular polity, the requirement of correct behaviour or propriety is that an appeal for votes should not be made on the ground of the candidate's religion which by itself is no index of the suitability of a candidate for membership of the House.' The soliciting of votes during an election on the grounds of a candidate's religion in a secular State was considered by the Court to be against the 'norms of decency and propriety of the society,' (ibid, para 30) and a provision restricting such activity constituted a reasonable fetter on the right to free expression.

provisions of the Representation of the People Act, 1951. The Court began by reviewing what it described as the relevant Supreme Court jurisprudence on the meaning of 'Hindu', 'Hinduism' and 'Hindutva'. After reviewing several cases on the meaning of 'Hindu' and 'Hinduism', the Court concluded that these Constitutional Bench decisions 'indicate that no precise meaning can be ascribed to the terms 'Hindu', 'Hindutva' and 'Hinduism' and no meaning in the abstract can confine it to the narrow limits of religion alone, excluding the content of Indian culture and heritage.'[10] On the meaning of Hindutva, the Court concluded:

> ...that the term 'Hindutva' is related more to *the way of life of the people in the subcontinent*. It is difficult to appreciate how in the face of these decisions the term 'Hindutva' or 'Hinduism' *per se*, in the abstract, can be assumed to mean and be equated with narrow fundamentalist Hindu religious bigotry, or be construed to fall within the prohibition in [section 123(3) or (3A)]. (emphasis added)[11]

In the Court's view, Hindutva is ordinarily to be understood 'as a way of life or state of mind and it is not to be equated with, or understood as religious Hindu fundamentalism.'[12] The words 'Hinduism' and 'Hindutva' should not be construed narrowly to refer only to the 'strict Hindu religious practices unrelated to the culture and ethos of the people of India'.[13] Rather, in the abstract, these terms should simply be seen to reflect the 'way of life of the Indian people'.[14] Accordingly, the Court concluded that simply referring to Hindutva or Hinduism in a speech does not automatically make it one based on the Hindu religion, and would not necessarily constitute an

[10] Ibid., p. 1129–30, para 38.
[11] Ibid., p. 1130, para 38.
[12] Ibid., p. 1130 para 40.
[13] Ibid., p. 1131, para 43.
[14] Ibid.

appeal to religion. Nor, in the Court's view, does such a reference necessarily 'depict an attitude hostile to all persons practising any religion other than the Hindu religion'.[15] Rather, it is the particular 'use made of these words and the meaning sought to be conveyed in the speech which has to be seen'.[16] Such words may be used in a speech 'to promote secularism or to emphasize the way of life of the Indian people and the Indian culture or ethos or to criticize the policy of any political party as discriminatory or intolerant'. The Court thus rejected the argument that the use of Hindutva *per se* necessarily constitutes a violation of sections 123(3) or (3A) of the Representation of the People Act, 1951. Instead, the Court was of the view that the question of whether a particular reference to Hindutva or Hinduism constitutes a violation of these sections must be a question of fact in each case.

On the facts of the case against Prabhoo and his agent, Thackeray, the Court found that Thackeray's speeches violated the Act. The passages at issue from Thackeray's speeches included some of the following: 'We are fighting this election for the protection of Hinduism. Therefore, we do not care for the votes of the Muslims. This country belongs to Hindus and will remain so';[17] 'Hinduism will triumph in this election and we must become honourable recipients of this victory to ward off the danger to Hinduism';[18] 'If anybody stands against Hindustan you should show courage by performing *pooja* (i.e. worship) with shoes... A candidate by name of Prabhoo should be led to victory in the name of religion';[19] 'We have come with

---

[15] Ibid., p. 1131, para 45.
[16] Ibid.
[17] Ibid., p. 1118, para 5
[18] Ibid., p. 1118–19, para 5.
[19] Ibid., p. 1119, para 5

the ideology of Hinduism. Shiv Sena will implement this ideology. Though this country belongs to Hindus, Ram and Krishna are insulted. (They) valued the Muslim vote more than your votes. We do not want the Muslim votes.'[20] In the Court's view, all of Thackeray's speeches constituted a clear appeal to the Hindu voters to vote for Prabhoo because he was a Hindu, and thus were in violation of section 123(3).[21] Further, the Court was of the view that one of Thackeray's speeches included derogatory references to Muslims that clearly amounted to an attempt to promote feelings of enmity and hatred between Hindus and Muslims, and were therefore in violation of section 123(3A). Thus, both Prabhoo and Thackeray were found guilty of corrupt practices. By way of contrast, in the case against Manohar Joshi, for a speech in which he stated that 'the first Hindu State will be established in Maharashtra', the Court held that Joshi was not guilty of violating section 123(3) or (3A).[22] Such a statement was not, in the Court's view, an appeal to votes on the basis of religion, but simply 'the expression, at best, of such a hope'.[23]

The outcome of other cases was similarly divided, though the tendency was to dismiss the convictions of the Bombay High Court. The conviction against Professor R. G. Kapse (an elected BJP candidate to the Lok Sabha), joined with notices against Pramod Mahajan and Sadhvi Rithambhara, was overturned by the Supreme Court. The speeches made by Mahajan and Rithambhara were not, in the Court's view, made with Kapse's consent. The fact that Rithambhara was present at and participated in a public meeting at which Kapse was allegedly present

---

[20] Ibid.

[21] Ibid., p. 1135, para 62.

[22] See Introduction n. 2, p. 816, para 60.

[23] Ibid.

could not be taken as consent to the content of those speeches.[24] Moreover, Kapse denied that he was even present at the meeting, and in the Court's view, there was no reliable evidence to prove his alleged conduct. The charges in relation to Mahajan's speech were similarly dismissed on evidentiary grounds, that is, there was not sufficient evidence to prove that he had used the words 'Hindutva' or 'Hindu religion' in his speeches, nor that he had raised the issue of the construction of the Ram temple in Ayodhya, or otherwise appealed to religion. The Court further held that the fact that these issues were raised in the BJP Manifesto was not sufficient to find an individual candidate guilty of corrupt practices. The charges against Shiv Sena candidate Ramakant Mayekar were also dismissed. The mere fact that Bal Thackeray, the leader of the Shiv Sena, was found guilty of corrupt practices was not in itself sufficient evidence to establish that other members of the party were also guilty of corrupt practices. Rather, a candidate's consent to the corrupt practices of the leader must be proven. In the Court's view, there was insufficient evidence to prove that the candidate had even been present at the speeches in question.[25]

By way of contrast, in the case of *Suryakant Venkatrao Mahadik v. Saroj Sandesh Naik*,[26] the Supreme Court held that the particular

[24] The notices against Rithambhara were also dismissed, on the basis that she had not been given notice as required under the Representation of the People Act, 1951 and thus denied the opportunity to defend herself against the allegation of corrupt practices.

[25] Again, on the question of the video tape which allegedly contained express appeals to Hindutva and the Hindu religion, the Court held that neither the content of the videos nor the candidate Ramakant Mayekar's consent to them, had been proven. The conviction against Chandrakanta Goyal, a BJP candidate, was dismissed on similar grounds: there was, in the Court's view, no direct evidence of the appellant's consent to the speeches of Thackeray or Mahajan.

[26] See n. 1 above.

use of the term 'Hindutva' *did* constitute a violation of section 123(3). Mahadik's speech 'was an appeal by a Hindu to a congregation of Hindu devotees in a Hindu temple during a Hindu religious festival with emphasis on the Hindu religion for giving votes to a Hindu candidate espousing the cause of the Hindu religion'.[27] In the Court's view, the use of the word 'Hindutva' in that speech 'at that time, place and occasion has to be understood only as an appeal on the ground of Hindu religion'. Following its holding in Prabhoo's case, the Court held that although in its general or abstract meaning, the word 'Hindutva' refers to the Indian culture and heritage, in this particular context it could only be interpreted as an appeal to religion.

A writ petition was subsequently brought, requesting that the Court reconsider its conclusions in the Hindutva case. The petition was rejected by the Court.[28] But in an attempt to clarify its decision, the Court made several further observations. First, the Court noted that there was nothing in the *Manohar Joshi* case that was inconsistent with the earlier decision of the Supreme Court in *Bommai v. Union of India*.[29] The *Bommai* case had involved a challenge to the validity of the presidential declaration dismissing the BJP governments in four states following the destruction of the mosque at Ayodhya and the ensuing communal riots. The Constitutional Bench of the Supreme Court upheld the validity of the declaration, and in so doing, passed considerable comment on the meaning of secularism in Indian constitutional law.[30] In the Hindutva

[27] Ibid., p. 99.

[28] See Introduction, n. 3. The Court stated that 'Article 32 of the Constitution is not available to assail the correctness of a decision on merits or to claim its reconsideration'. In the Court's view, this alone was sufficient to dismiss the writ petition.

[29] Chapter 1, n. 13.

[30] For a further discussion, see chapter 4.

review petition, counsel argued that the Supreme Court's comments on secularism in *Bommai* were inconsistent with the Supreme Court's conclusion in the Hindutva case. But, the Court hearing the review petition disagreed. In its view, *Bommai* did not relate to the interpretation of sections 3 and 3(A) of the Representation of the People Act, 1951, 'and therefore nothing in the decision in *Bommai* is of assistance for construing the meaning and scope' of those sections of the Act. Any reference to the *Bommai* decision was thus, in the Court's words, 'inapposite in this context'. The Court further commented that the challenge in the writ petition to the correctness of the *Manohar Joshi* decision was 'based on misreading of that decision'. Rather, the decision was simply based on earlier Constitution Bench decisions of the Supreme Court, which the Court was bound to follow. In its view, 'a careful and dispassionate reading of the decision would show that the apprehensions and misgivings expressed in the writ petition are imaginary and baseless'. According to the Court, there was nothing in the judgment to give rise to the fear that it had in any way condoned the appeal to religion to gain votes in an election. Although the Court's emphasis that it did not sanction an appeal to religion in electoral politics was a welcome one, the Court failed to address the fundamental contradictions in the *Manohar Joshi* decision, and in fact may only have intensified these contradictions. In our view, the Court erred in the original decisions on two significant points—the interpretation of the meaning of Hindutva, and the secular nature of the speeches of the Hindu Right. In the sections that follow, we take a closer look at these particular dimensions of the Hindutva decision, and reveal the dangerous implications of the errors made by the Court.

3

Vindicating Hindutva

'The apex Court has fully and unambiguously endorsed the concept of Hindutva which the [BJP] has been propounding since its inception.'

Organiser, Editorial, December 24, 1995

The Supreme Court decision was immediately claimed by the Hindu Right as a vindication of their vision of Hindutva.[1] The front page of the December 24th edition of the *Organiser*, a newspaper that serves as the English-language mouthpiece of the RSS, proudly declared 'Triumph of

[1] The *Organiser* is a weekly English language newspaper published by the Hindu Right. See the following articles in the *Organiser*: 'Triumph of Truth' (cover story) and 'Satyameva Jayate' (editorial) Dec 24, 1995, p. 2; 'Cultural Nationalism Wins Over Pseudo-secularism' Dec 24, 1995, p. 3; 'Hindutva is the Soul of India'—H. V. Seshadri Dec 31, 1995, p. 7; Justice Guman Mal Lodha, 'Reference to Establishment of Hindu State is not a Religious Appeal, Dec 31, 1995, p. 7; 'Hindutva, a uniting force' Jan 7, 1996, p. 16; M. Rama Josi, 'SC Judgment on Hindutva Flawless' Jan 21, 1996, p. 2; 'Arise, Awake, Act: H. V. Seshadri's Address Mar 8, 1996' Mar 17, 1996, p. 9; and Jagmohan, 'Hinduism, Hindutva and the Supreme Court' Mar 31, 1996, p. 8.

Truth', and several articles in the edition waxed eloquently on the decisive victory that the judgment represented for the forces of Hindutva and Hindu Rashtra.[2] One article trumpeted: 'The Supreme Court has put its seal of judicial imprimatur on the Sangh ideology of Hindutva by stating that it is a way of life or state of mind and that it is not to be equated with or understood as religious fundamentalism.' H. V. Seshadri, leader of the RSS, welcomed the judgment as 'a vindication of the philosophy of Hindu Rashtra'.[3] Conversely, the Supreme Court's comments on Hindutva came under immediate fire from those committed to democratic secularism. In this section, we take a closer look at the Supreme Court reasoning on the meaning of Hindutva. In our view, there is good reason to be concerned about the conclusions reached by the Court. First, the conclusions are unsupported on the face of the decision itself, that is, the Court did not provide any evidentiary basis (factual nor expert) nor any precedential authority for its conclusion. Second, we argue that the Court could not do so precisely because the conclusion is inconsistent with the historic and contemporary political meaning of the term Hindutva.

'A WAY OF LIFE' WITHOUT PRECEDENT

In reaching its conclusions on the meaning of Hindutva, the Supreme Court quoted extensively from two earlier decisions of the Constitutional Bench of the Supreme Court. The first, *Sastri Yagnaparushadji and Others v. Muldas Bhudardas Vaishya*

[2] See *Organiser*, Dec 24, 1995, ibid.

[3] Ibid., p. 3. See also *Organiser*, Dec 31, 1995, p. 7. 'Hindutva is the Soul of India', wherein H. V. Seshadri further responded to the Supreme Court judgment, stating that the decision reflects '...the very broad and all-embracing concept of Hindutva that the RSS and the RSS-inspired organizations have been propagating'.

and Another,[4] involved a lengthy discussion on who and what are Hindus, which passed considerable comment on the meaning of Hinduism:

Unlike other religions in the world, the *Hindu religion* does not claim any one prophet; it does not worship any one God; it does not subscribe to any one dogma; it does not believe in any one philosophic concept; it does not follow any one set of religious rites or performances; in fact, it does not appear to satisfy the narrow traditional features of any religion or creed. *It may broadly be described as a way of life and nothing more*...When we consider this broad sweep of the Hindu philosophic concepts, it would be realized that under Hindu philosophy there is no scope for ex-communicating any notion or principle as heretical and rejecting it as such... Hinduism takes it for granted that there is more than one valid approach to truth and to salvation and these different approaches are not only compatible with each other, but are complementary.[5] [emphasis added]

The second case, *Commr. of Wealth Tax, Madras, and Ors. v. Late R. Sridharan by L.R.s*,[6] also involved a considerable discussion of the meaning of Hinduism:[7]

It is a matter of common knowledge that Hinduism embraces within self [sic] so many diverse forms of beliefs, faiths, practices and worship that it is difficult to define the term 'Hindu' with precision.[8]

[4] 1966 (3) SCR 242.

[5] *Prabhoo*, chapter 2, n. 1, p. 1127, para 36. For a detailed analysis of this decision, see Marc Galanter 'Hinduism, Secularism and the Indian Judiciary' in Rajeev Bhargava, ed., *Secularism and its Critics*, 1998.

[6] (1976) Supp SCR 478.

[7] The decision included various dictionary and encyclopaedia definitions of Hinduism. For example, Webster's International Dictionary defined Hinduism as: '...a complex body of social, cultural and religious beliefs and practices evolved in and largely confined to the Indian subcontinent, an outlook tending to view all forms and theories as aspects of one eternal being and truth', (*Prabhoo*, see chapter 2, n. 1, p. 1129 para 37). The passage from the case also referred to definitions in the Encyclopaedia Britannica and the work of B. G. Tilak.

[8] Ibid., p. 1129, para 37.

But the passages cited from the *Sridharan* case further elaborated on the nature of Hinduism, which it defined as 'incorporat(ing) all forms of belief and worship without necessitating the selection or elimination of any. The Hindu is inclined to revere the divine in every manifestation, whatever it may be, is doctrinally tolerant, leaving others—including both Hindus and non-Hindus—whatever creed and worship practices suit them best.'[9]

Based on these two decisions, the Court in Prabhoo concluded that no precise meaning could be given to the words 'Hindu', 'Hinduism' or 'Hindutva':

...no meaning in the abstract can confine it to the narrow limits of religion alone, excluding the content of Indian culture and heritage. It is also indicated that the term 'Hindutva' is related more to the way of life of the people in the sub-continent. It is difficult to appreciate how in the face of these decisions the term 'Hindutva' or 'Hinduism' per se, in the abstract, can be assumed to mean and be equated with narrow fundamentalist Hindu religious bigotry, or...fall within the prohibition of...section 123 of the Representation of the People Act.[10]

There are a number of troubling dimensions to this conclusion. First, in the Court's view, even the term 'Hinduism' cannot be given any precise meaning, and is not limited to 'the narrow confines of religion'. Rather, even the word 'Hinduism' is seen to reflect 'the way of life of the Indian people'. Although the Court's conclusion that 'Hinduism' ought not to be reduced to 'or equated with narrow fundamentalist Hindu religious bigotry' is uncontentious, its conclusion that Hinduism ought not to be confined to religion at all is highly contentious, and in our view, erroneous. The very definitions cited by the Court in *Sridharan* all point to the common understanding of Hinduism as a religion, albeit one that embraces a multiplicity of gods, texts and religious rites.

[9] Ibid., p. 1129, para 37.
[10] Ibid., pp 1129–30, para 38.

Yet even more troubling are the Court's conclusions on the meaning of Hindutva. What the Court does not mention, nor does it seem to be remotely troubled by, is the fact that neither of these two decisions of the Constitutional Bench so much as mentioned the word 'Hindutva'. The Court nevertheless goes on to elaborate on the meaning of Hindutva as 'the way of life or state of mind of the people of the sub-continent', a meaning that it derives from the two decisions dealing with the meaning of 'Hinduism'. In further support of its conclusions that Hindutva represents a 'way of life', and not simply 'religious Hindu fundamentalism', the Court then quoted a passage from the work of Maulana Wahiduddin Khan (1994):

The strategy worked out to solve the minorities problem was, although differently worded, that of Hindutva or Indianization. This strategy, briefly stated, aims at developing a uniform culture by obliterating the differences between all of the cultures co-existing in the country. This was felt to be the way to communal harmony and national unity. It was thought that this would put an end once and for all to the minorities problem.[11]

This passage is cited by the Court to support the conclusion that 'the word "Hindutva" is used and understood as a synonym of "Indianization" i.e., the development of uniform culture by obliterating the differences between all the cultures co-existing in the country.'[12] What the Court does not mention, nor does it seem to be in any way troubled by, is the fact that the passage quoted is a description of a particular strategy worked out by a particular political party—the Bharatiya Jana Sangh, the ideological precursor of the BJP. Although their discourse did equate Hindutva with Indianization, this equation within the

[11] Ibid., p. 1130 para 40 citing Khan, *Indian Muslims: Need for a Positive Outlook* (1994).
[12] Ibid.

political rhetoric of the Hindu Right is hardly comforting. It should, on the contrary, be considerable cause for concern. The Court, however, does not interrogate the strategy of Indianization. It did not consider what was involved in the creation of a uniform culture (i.e. a Hindu culture), nor the obliteration of differences (i.e. of Muslim religion/identity). Rather, it simply deploys the passage as an authority for the proposition that Hindutva is synonymous with Indianization, and by taking the passage out of context, the Court uses it as further support for its view that Hindutva is simply a way of life of the Indian people.

The Court subsequently quoted at length from *Kultar Singh v. Mukhtiar Singh*,[13] another decision of the Constitutional Bench of the Supreme Court, which held that a poster which contained the word 'Panth' did not constitute an appeal to votes on the basis of religion, since the word 'panth' did not mean the Sikh religion. The Court was of the view that the *Kultar Singh* case stood for the proposition that the word in dispute should not be considered 'in the abstract, but in the context of its use'.[14] The Court once again reiterated its basic conclusion:

Thus, it cannot be doubted, particularly in view of the Constitution Bench decisions of this Court that the words 'Hinduism' or 'Hindutva' are not necessarily to be understood and construed narrowly, confined only to the strict Hindu religious practices unrelated to the culture and ethos of the people of India, depicting the way of life of the Indian people. Unless the context of a speech indicates a contrary meaning or use, in the abstract these terms are indicative more of a way of life of the Indian people and are not confined merely to describe persons practising the Hindu religion as a faith.[15]

---

[13] 1964 (7) SCR 790.
[14] Prabhoo, see chapter 2, n. 1, p. 1131 para 42.
[15] Ibid., p. 1131, para 43.

The Court further emphasized that there was nothing inherent in the terms 'Hinduism' or 'Hindutva' that depicts any hostility, enmity or intolerance to any other religious community. Although the terms may have been misused by some to promote communalism, such misuse does not change 'the true meaning of these terms'.[16] Returning to the issue at hand, the Court then concluded that mere references to the words 'Hinduism' or 'Hindutva' in a speech does not constitute a violation of either s.123(3) or s.123(3A) of the Representation of the People Act, 1951. Rather, it is 'the kind of use made of these words and the meaning sought to be conveyed in each particular speech which must be considered'.[17] The issue, then, of the violation of the Act becomes a question of fact in each case.

What is most extraordinary about the Court's reasoning, from a strictly legal point of view, is that it can draw such an unequivocal conclusion as to the meaning of Hindutva without having cited virtually any authorities—judicial or otherwise—in its support. None of the Constitutional Bench decisions from which it purported to draw support addressed the meaning of the term 'Hindutva', but simply the meaning of 'Hindu' or 'Hinduism'. The Supreme Court takes no notice of the possibility that these terms may not in fact converge, but proceeds from the assumption that their meaning can be conflated, and thus infers the meaning of one (Hindutva) from the other (Hinduism). Hindutva and Hinduism are taken to mean the same thing. Since Hinduism is not, in the Court's view, an appeal to religion, then neither is Hindutva. And since Hinduism is not an expression of enmity towards religious minorities, then neither is Hindutva. Rather, since Hinduism is taken to mean the way of life of the people of the subcontinent, then

[16] Ibid., p. 1131 para 44.
[17] Ibid., p. 1131, para 45.

so too does Hindutva. In reaching these conclusions, the Court has made in our view two critical mistakes. First, it has collapsed the meaning of Hinduism and Hindutva. Secondly, and relatedly, in order to be able to conclude that Hindutva is not an appeal to religion, the Court was forced to take the position that Hinduism is not an appeal to religion (in apparent conflict with earlier Supreme Court decisions which appear to recognize that Hinduism is a religion). As we will argue in the next section, the relationship between Hinduism and Hindutva is rather more complex. Although these terms should not be conflated, we will attempt to reveal the extent to which Hindutva is in fact an appeal to the Hindu religion.

The Supreme Court's conclusion on the meaning of Hindutva further exemplifies the way in which the unstated norms of the majority come to be inscribed in legal principles. Hinduism, the religion of the majority of Indians, comes to reflect the way of life of *all* Indians. Hindutva, similarly abstracted from the religion of the majority, also becomes the way of life of *all* the people of the subcontinent. The Court uncritically assumes that the norms of the majority can simply be extended to apply to all Indians; regardless of their religious or cultural identity. Similarly, 'Indianization' is taken by the Court to represent the political and cultural aspirations of all Indians, in and through the construction of a uniform culture. The Court does not stop to consider that this uniform culture is one based on assimilating religious and cultural minorities, and on reconstituting all Indian citizens in the image of the unstated dominant norm, that is, a Hindu norm. The Court simply assumes, rather than in any way critically interrogating, that majoritarian norms are the appropriate measure against which the practices and rhetoric of the Hindu Right can be judged. Although there is nothing particularly extraordinary about the Court's implicit reliance on unstated dominant norms—judicial reasoning more often than not does incorporate these assumptions—the implications of these norms for religious and cultural minorities who deviate from them can be very damaging. As we will also attempt to reveal in the sections that follow, the implications of these unstated norms of the Hindu majority in the Supreme Court's conclusions on Hindutva are particularly devastating for these minorities, who are the very targets of the Hindu Right.

HINDUTVA AND THE HINDU RIGHT

By concluding that the term 'Hindutva' was not in and of itself an appeal to religion, nor an expression of enmity or hatred towards other religious groups, but simply the way of life of Indian people, the Supreme Court has obscured the historical background as well as the contemporary political context within which the term has acquired meaning. As several commentators have pointed out, the Court failed to recognize that the term 'Hindutva' has historically had a very particular meaning, associated with the political philosophy of two early leaders of the Hindu Right, namely Vir Savarkar and M. S. Golwalkar, and the political agenda of the Hindu Right.[18] A brief review of their writings on Hindutva and Hindu Rashtra reveals that

[18] See, for example, Anil Nauriya 'The Hindutva Judgments: A Warning Signal', *EPW*, Jan 10, 1996, who argues that the Court has failed 'to recognise that Hindutva as an expression has a special meaning and is associated with the social and political philosophy of Savarkar and Golwalkar, that is, the Hindu Mahasabha and the RSS', p. 11. For a general discussion of the concept of Hindutva in the writings of the Hindu Right, see Rizwan Qaiser, 'The Conceptualisation of Communalism and Hindu Rashtra', in Rudolf C. Heredia and Edward Mathias (eds.), *Secularism And Liberation: Perspectives And Strategies For India Today* (1995). Rizwan Qaiser has traced the history of the term 'Hindu Rashtra' and 'Hindutva'. He argues that initially the term 'Hindu Rashtra' had no communal overtones, but was a strategy of resistance

these terms are both an appeal to religion and an expression of enmity to religious minorities.

The contemporary meaning of Hindutva has its roots in the writings of Savarkar, particularly in his pamphlet 'Hindutva: Who is a Hindu?' written in 1923.[19] In first articulating the concepts of Hindutva and Hinduness as political concepts, Savarkar emphasized that 'Hindutva is different from Hinduism'.

Hindutva is not identical with what is vaguely indicated by the term Hinduism. By an 'ism' is generally meant a theory or a code more or less based on spiritual or religious dogma or system. But when we attempt to investigate into the essential significance of Hindutva we do not primarily—and certainly not mainly—concern ourselves with any particular theocratic or religious dogma or creed. Had not linguistic usage stood in our way then 'Hinduness' would have certainly been a better word than Hinduism as a near parallel to Hindutva. Hindutva embraces all the departments of thought and activity of the whole being of our Hindu role.[20]

---

to British colonial rule and cultural domination. However, in the 1930s and 1940s, certain Hindu organizations wanted to establish a Hindu Rashtra, that could involve a total subjugation of all non-Hindus to a 'master' race. Qaiser points out that the main exponents for this version of a Hindu Rashtra were V. D. Savarkar, Shyama Prasad Mookerjee and M. S. Golwalkar. He describes their conceptualization of a Hindu Rashtra as follows: 'Firstly, all Hindus were one entity culturally and politically; secondly the interests of all the Hindus was the same, which could be jeopardized if they were not united; thirdly, the Muslims were the biggest threat to the Hindu interest, therefore necessitating the sharpest hostility towards them in political as well as cultural terms' (p. 100).

[19] V. D. Savarkar, *Hindutva: Who Is A Hindu?*, (1929), (4th Edition, S. P. Gokhale 1949). Savarkar was the ideological leader of the Hindu nationalists and later became leader of the Hindu Mahasabha, a Hindu communalist party that was intensely involved in the Independence struggle. His writings on Hindutva continue to represent the ideological foundations of the contemporary Hindu Right.

[20] Ibid., pp 3–4.

In rather striking contrast to the Supreme Court decision, Savarkar began by positing the concept of Hindutva as something distinct from Hinduism and as a means for achieving superiority of the Hindu race, rather than the religion. According to Savarkar, 'Hindus are not merely the citizens of the Indian state because they are united not only by the bonds of love they bear to a common motherland but also by the bonds of a common blood... All Hindus claim to have in their veins the blood of the mighty race incorporated with and descended from the Vedic forefathers'.[21] In this definition, a Hindu is thus cast in racial terms.[22] But Savarkar did not stop at this concept of a common fatherland and a common racial bond. Rather, for him, a Hindu was also one who inherits Indian civilization 'as represented in a common history, common heroes, a common literature, a common art, a common law and a common jurisprudence, common fairs and festivals, rites and rituals, ceremonies and sacraments'.[23] Hindus were thus defined in terms of their common cultural heritage.

Again, Savarkar did not stop here. A Hindu was further defined as one who followed 'the religion of the people peculiar and native to this land' namely Hinduism. In Savarkar's definition a Hindu is a 'person who regards the land of Bharatvarsha from Indus to the Seas as his Fatherland as well as his Holyland—that is the cradle of his religion'.[24] A Hindu

[21] Ibid., p. 68.

[22] As Purushottam Agarwal has argued in 'Savarkar, Surat and Draupadi', in *Women and the Hindu Right*, see Introduction, n. 1, p. 41, 'Savarkar was by no means the first to attempt a racial reconstruction of the traditional religious community. But he was undoubtedly the most articulate. It was in his discourse that attempts to theoretically construct a Hindu political community which shared the same racial bonds and historical memories came into shape.'

[23] Savarkar, *Who Is A Hindu?*, p. 81.

[24] Ibid., pp 3–4.

is thus one whose fatherland (*pitribhumi*) and holyland (*punyabhumi*) correspond. It is through this elision of fatherland and holyland that Savarkar constructs the political category of Hindu in opposition to non-Hindus, particularly to Muslims and Christians. Despite the fact that Muslims and Christians 'have inherited along with Hindus a common Fatherland and a greater part of the wealth of common culture—language, law, custom, folklore and history, [they] are not and cannot be recognized as Hindus... Their Holyland is far off in Arabia or Persia'.[25] The construction of a 'Hindu race' was thus achieved by continuously positing a conflict between the 'Hindu' and 'others', most notably, the 'Muslim invader'.[26]

Although Savarkar was emphatic that Hindutva was distinct from Hinduism, it was also clear in his writings that Hinduism was an important part of being Hindu. As Purushottam Agarwal has argued, Savarkar effectively transforms the role of religion in constituting the category of Hindu: 'In religious discourse the community is defined in terms of a shared creed or dogma. In the political discourse of communalism, the community is defined primarily as a race. Religion, instead of being a defining criterion, is transformed into a fetish owned by an already

---

[25] Ibid., p. 92.

[26] In Savarkar's words, '... in this prolonged furious conflict our people became intensely conscious of ourselves as Hindus and were welded into a nation to an extent unknown in our history...' Ibid., p. 45. Mookerjee's concept of a Hindu Rashtra was slightly distinct from Savarkar's according to Qaiser. Mookerjee was concerned about the humiliation of Hindus and Bengal amid the failure of the Congress party to defend Hindu rights. He subsequently joined Savarkar as a member of the All India Hindu Mahasabha and began to adopt the communal rhetoric of Savarkar. While Savarkar's preoccupation was with the threat of Muslim rule, Mookerjee used the concept of Hindu Rashtra primarily to describe how the Hindus alone would liberate the country from British rule.

defined community'.[27] Hindus, according to Savarkar, were a race who by definition followed a particular religion. And by definition, Hindus were constituted in opposition to Muslims and Christians whose very identities were constituted as always posing a threat of disloyalty. Although Muslims and Christians were also constituted in racial terms, it was clear that the threat that they posed lay in the fact that their holyland was other than in India. Again, despite the emphasis on racial differences, it was the difference of religion that remained as a constituting moment of the oppositional identities.

The definition of Hindu Rashtra was further articulated in the writings of Golwalkar.[28] Golwalkar's vision of a Hindu nation included five components:

The idea contained in the word Nation is a compound of five distinct factors fused into one indissoluble whole the famous five unities: Geographical (country), Racial (race), Religious (religion), Cultural (culture) and Linguistic (language).[29]

Golwalkar elaborated in considerable detail the meaning he ascribed to each of these categories. Country is described as 'hereditary territory... relating to which [a people] have certain indissoluble bonds of community'.[30] A race is defined as 'a

[27] Agarwal, see above n. 22, p. 40.

[28] The word Hindutva does not appear in Golwalkar's English language publications. Rather, the terms 'Hindu Nation', 'Hindu culture', 'Hindu people', 'Hindu life' appear throughout the text. It is worth noting however that most of Golwalkar's writings and speeches were in Hindi and only subsequently translated into English. Without a more detailed analysis of his Hindi texts, we are unable to comment further on the significance of the absence of the term 'Hindutva' from the English translations. Nevertheless, Golwalkar's articulation of the components of the Hindu Nation/Rashtra remain crucial to an understanding of the contemporary deployment of the ideology of the Hindutva by the Hindu Right.

[29] M. S. Golwalkar, *We Or Our Nationhood Defined* (1939), p. 18.

[30] Ibid., p. 20.

hereditary society having common customs, common language, common memories of glory or disaster; in short, it is a population with a common origin under one culture.'[31] Religion and culture are defined together, because in Golwalkar's view, the two are often indistinguishable:

Where religion forms the very life-breath of a people, where it governs every action of the individual as well as of the society as a whole, where in short, it forms the only incentive to all action, worldly and spiritual, it is difficult to distinguish these two factors.[32]

In elaborating on his definition of religion, Golwalkar argued that those who say that religion has no place in politics fail to understand the real meaning of religion:

Religion, in its essence is that which by regulating society in all its functions, makes room for all individual idiosyncrasies, and provides suitable ways and means for all sorts of mental frames to adopt, and evolve and which at the same time raises the whole society as such, from the material through the moral to the spiritual plane.[33]

In his view, this religion 'cannot be ignored in individual or in public life'.[34] Finally, language is defined as an essential characteristic belonging to every nation: 'Every race, living in its own country, evolves a language of its own, reflecting its culture, its religion, its history and tradition'.[35]

Golwalkar argued that the Hindus qualify under each of these categories, and thus, constitute a nation. 'Hindustan, the land of the Hindus...a definite geographical unity' constitutes a country. '[T]he Hindu Race is united together by common traditions, ...memories, ...culture, ...language,

[31] Ibid., p. 21.
[32] Ibid., p. 21.
[33] Ibid., p. 23.
[34] Ibid.
[35] Ibid., p. 26.

...[and] customs', and thus constitutes a race.[36] On religion and culture:

This great Hindu Race professes its illustrious Hindu Religion, the only religion in the world worthy of being so denominated, which in its variety is still an organic whole... Guided by this Religion in all walks of life, individual, social, political, the Race evolved a culture which despite the degenerating contact with the debased 'civilisations' of the Mussalmans and the Europeans, for the last ten centuries, is still the noblest in the world.[37]

In Golwalkar's view 'No race is more fortunate in being given a Religion, which could produce such a culture'.[38] On the question of language, he recognized a problem, in so far as it appears that each region has its own language. But, he argued 'there is but one language, Sanskrit, of which these many languages are mere offshoots'.[39] Thus, Golwalkar concluded, 'this country, Hindustan, the Hindu Race with its Hindu Religion, Hindu Culture, and Hindu Language, complete the Nation concept'.[40]

In this definition, although religion is but one of the five qualifying categories of the Hindu Nation, it can be seen to underlie the other four categories. Race is defined not so much in terms of a common blood line (as in Savarkar's definition), as it is in terms of a common culture. It is less a biological category than a cultural one, and culture is in turn defined almost wholly in terms of a common religion, since in Golwalkar's view, religion and culture for the Hindus are virtually indistinguishable. Thus, both race and culture are constituted in and through the category of religion. Despite the

[36] Ibid., p. 40.
[37] Ibid., p. 41.
[38] Ibid., p. 42.
[39] IIbid., p. 43.
[40] Ibid., p. 43.

efforts to insist that the category of Hindu is broader than that of Hinduism, we can begin to see that the religion of Hinduism remains the constituting moment of this broader political category. The other two categories—of country and language—can in turn be seen to be derivative of this religious category. Country is simply the geographical territory where a people united by religion/culture/race live, and language, similarly, that which a people united by religion/culture/race, speak. The priority of religion within this construct of religion/culture/race reveals that, despite Golwalkar's efforts to insist on the distinct nature of the five categories, it is in fact the common religion of Hinduism from which the entire definition of the Hindu Nation is derived. The appeal for a Hindu Nation is thus very much an appeal to religion.

The primacy of religion is further evident in Golwalkar's discussion of the 'problem' of those who live in Hindustan, but who are not part of the Hindu race, religion and culture, namely the Muslims and Christians. In his view, those who were not a part of the Hindu Race, still had a chance to be a part of the Hindu Nation if certain conditions were met:

All those...can have no place in the national life, unless they abandon their differences, adopt the religion, culture and language of the Nation and completely merge themselves in the National Race. So long, however, as they maintain their racial, religious and cultural differences, they cannot but be only foreigners.., the strangers have to acknowledge the National religion as the State Religion and in every other respect inseparably merge in the National community.[41]

Although Muslims and Christians are cast as 'foreign races', the constituting moment of this racial category remains one of religion. As in Savarkar's writings, the problem with these minorities is not that they do not share a common land, a

[41] Ibid., pp 45–6.

common language, or even part of a common culture. The real problem lies with the absence of the requisite 'mental allegiance': a mental allegiance that Muslims and Christians have not demonstrated. It is the fact that Muslims and Christians do not look upon India as their holy land, and thus continue to display a *religious* allegiance to a foreign land that is of concern to Golwalkar. The call on these communities to 'give up their present foreign mental complexion and merge in the common stream of our national life',[42] is thus a call to give up their religion, which lies other than in the Hindu nation. Despite the fact that Golwalkar speaks of racial and cultural differences, these differences only make sense in relation to the underlying category of religion. The call for assimilation is thus, first and foremost, a call for religious assimilation; for minorities to return to the folds of Hinduism. It is only secondarily a call to assimilate into the culture and race, in so far as this culture and race is one that is derivative of the religious category.

Moreover, it is in these discussions of the minorities that we can again see the extent to which the political category of 'Hindu' has been constituted in opposition to religious minorities, and premised on the very elimination of these minorities, through assimilation or considerably more violent means. Religious minorities are constituted in this discourse as presenting a threat to the integrity of the Nation, and could not be recognized or accommodated as a legitimate part of the Hindu Nation. Golwalkar was very clear that there was no place for religious minorities who failed to assimilate: they must 'lose their separate existence to merge in the Hindu race, or may stay in the country, wholly subordinated to the Hindu Nation, claiming nothing, deserving no privileges, far less any preferential treatment—*not even citizen's rights*'[43] [emphasis

[42] M. S. Golwalkar, *Bunch of Thoughts*, (1966), p. 130.
[43] See above, n. 29, pp 47–8.

added]. The Hindu Nation was thus constituted in the writings of Golwalkar through an attack on the very legitimacy of religious minorities, and on a denial of any protection of minority rights within the Hindu Nation. The appeal for a Hindu Nation was thus also very much an expression of enmity to religious minorities.

These conceptualizations of the Hindu Nation continue to inform the political agenda of the Hindu Right today. Hindutva means establishing a Hindu Rashtra—a Hindu state, based on a Hindu way of life. As Savarkar did before them, the contemporary ideologues of the Hindu Right continue to emphasize a distinction between Hindu and Hinduism, and like Golwalkar before them, they continue to insist that Hindu is an attitude of allegiance. For example, Seshadri writes:

Hindu is not the name of a religious faith like the 'Muslim' or the 'Christian'. It denotes a national way of life here. All those who feel firmly committed to the unity and sanctity of our country and our people and look upon our great forebearers as their national heroes and the sublime values of our cultural life as their points of veneration and emulation are all Hindus.[44]

Yet, despite this continued emphasis that Hindu means more than the 'ism' of Hinduism, it remains all too evident that the constituting moment of Hinduness is still religion. Hinduism continues to be the religion followed by the Hindus, and it continues to be asserted as the only religion worthy of the name. It is time and again asserted as the only religion premised on the notion of toleration, which is in turn used to justify the claim that only Hindus are truly secular.[45] The supremacy of Hinduism remains the basis of the political claims against the

[44] H. V. Seshadri, *The Way*, (1991), p. 55.

[45] For a discussion of the Hindu Right's position that Hinduism is the only truly secular religion since it alone is based on toleration, see chapter 4, notes pp 69–73.

minorities, who follow religions that allow neither toleration nor secularism. While the political category of Hindu continues to be given precedence, Hinduism nevertheless remains as a crucial dimension of this category.

Indeed, if anything, the salience of religion in the discourse of the Hindu Right has only increased since the advent of the VHP. Indeed, the emphasis on Hindu as a racial rather than a religious category, and the distinction between Hindu and Hinduism has begun to blur with the rise of the VHP within the Hindu Right. The VHP is an organization explicitly committed to promoting Hinduism. Moreover, it claims to represent the totality of Hinduism; in effect, it attempts to reconstitute Hinduism as an organized religion under its central auspices. As Basu, et al. have argued, this appeal to religion in and through the VHP has been part of the phase of popularizing Hindutva; that is, of moving beyond the elite cells of the RSS *shakhas* and popularizing the message of Hindutva among the Hindu masses.[46] It is within this context of popularizing Hindutva that the campaign to construct a Ram temple in Ayodhya acquired such importance and dynamism within the Hindu Right. It is, moreover, within the context of this campaign that the religious nature of the political rhetoric of the Hindu Right has become most evident. The ascendance of the Ram legend, as well as the political mobilization of large numbers of 'holymen' (sants and sadhus) into the popular front of the Hindu Right has given it a distinctly religious flavour. Although traces of the racial construction of Hindus remain in evidence, particularly in the ongoing attacks on the Muslim community, the VHP is unapologetic in its emphasis on religion.

[46] See Basu *et al.*, chapter 1, n. 2.

In its contemporary deployment, the subtle distinction between Hindu, Hindutva and Hinduism of earlier times is often lost. The political discourse is imbued with religious discourse, at times espousing the superiority of Hinduism, at others, simply punctuating political appeals with the language, symbols and ceremonies of Hinduism. But the relationship between Hindu as a political category and Hinduism as a religious category remains complex. For example, the explicitly religious claims of the VHP to represent an already existing collectivity of Hindus only makes sense in relation to the underlying conceptualization of Hindu as a racial category.[47] Moreover, while the appeal to religion has grown, the concept of Hindu Rashtra and Hindutva does continue to mean more than an appeal to the religion of Hinduism. For the Hindu Right, an equally important dimension of Hindutva continues to be the attack on the legitimacy of minority rights. Hindutva continues to mean the assimilation of all minorities into the culture, way of life, ultimately the religion, of the majority. The concept of Hindutva thus retains its oppositional meaning; that is, it continues to be constituted largely in relation to that which it opposes—namely Muslims and Christians. The attack on the legitimacy of minority religious communities continues to go to the very core of the concept of Hindu Rashtra and Hindutva. From Savarkar to Golwalkar to the contemporary ideologues, it is this attack on religious minorities, on the effort to assimilate these minorities back into the folds of Hinduism, that has given Hindutva its political character. The current phase of popularizing the agenda of the Hindu Right through the VHP retains this essentially political attack on religious minorities. The appeal to religion has not fundamentally altered this character, but simply popularized it through the invocation of religious discourse.

[47] Nauriya, see above n. 18.

In the contemporary political terrain, Hindutva thus continues to be a political category that is distinct from the religion of Hinduism, but which relies on religion in constituting the political category of Hindu. The Supreme Court has completely failed to understand the meaning of the term, and its complex relationship to the religion of Hinduism.[48] For the Court to infer the meaning of Hindutva simply from reviewing its jurisprudence on the meaning of Hinduism and Hindu is simply inaccurate. At the same time, for the Court to conclude that an appeal to Hindutva is not *per se* an appeal to religion is to also misrepresent the complex relationship between these terms in the contemporary strategies of the Hindu Right. Although the concept of Hindutva has developed as distinct from Hinduism, it is a concept that nevertheless presupposes the religion of its constituency. Moreover in recent years, the political usage of the term has become more and more imbued with explicitly religious discourse. When used in the context of electoral politics, Hindutva is an appeal to religion, and as such, ought to constitute a violation of section 123(3) of the Representation of the People Act, 1951.

Secondly, Hindutva continues to be a political category that at its core is an attack on the legitimacy of minority rights. For the Court to conclude that there is nothing inherent in the concept of Hindutva that involves the promotion of religious enmity, hatred or disharmony is, again, simply inaccurate. The

---

[48] The historical use of the term 'Indianization' is similarly obscured in the Supreme Court judgment. The Court fails to recognise that the term was used by Jana Sangh leaders in the 1960s who directed it at the Muslims, and that it contained the insinuation that they were not Indian enough. For the court to suggest that 'Hindutva' is merely to be understood as a synonym of 'Indianization', therefore, contains an element of truth quite different from what the court may have had in mind; it is such a synonym but principally in the RSS discourse. Nauriya, above n. 18, p. 11.

Supreme Court has failed to understand the assault on religious minorities that is a constituent element of the concept of Hindutva. From its roots in the writings of Savarkar to its contemporary deployment by the likes of Bal Thackeray, Manohar Joshi, Sadhvi Rithambhara and L. K. Advani, Hindutva has been based on the idea of Indian society fractured by the conflict between religious communities, particularly between the Hindus and Muslims, wherein the majority of Hindus have been and continue to be oppressed at the hands of the Muslim minority. Hindutva is a call to unite against these religious minorities. At best, it is a call to assimilate these minorities into the ostensibly more tolerant fabric of Hinduism; and at its more extreme, it is a call simply to destroy them. In both its more modest assimilationist mode and in its more extreme and violent mode, Hindutva is an attack on the rights, indeed on the very legitimacy of religious minorities. As a call to assimilate or otherwise undermine the very identity and integrity of minority communities, it is based on a total disregard and lack of respect for other religious groups. As such, its political deployment can only be seen as promoting enmity, disharmony, and often hatred between religious groups. The Supreme Court has simply failed to understand the political agenda that informs the meaning of Hindutva in the contemporary political landscape, where an appeal to Hindutva is both an appeal to religion, and an appeal promoting enmity and hatred between religious groups. When used in the context of electoral politics, Hindutva ought to constitute a violation of both sections 123(3) and 123(3A) of the Representation of the People Act, 1951.

For the Hindu Right, Hindutva is indeed a way of life—a way of life of the Hindus who, by definition, practise Hinduism. It is not about the way of life of the Muslims or the Christians in India. For the Hindu Right, Hindutva is about the assimilation and ultimate negation of these religious minorities. This is the meaning of Hindutva both in its historic and contemporary context. It is in this light that the Supreme Court's conclusions that Hindutva simply represents 'a way of life of the people of the subcontinent' must be evaluated and ultimately, rejected. Hindutva is *not* the way of life of all the people of the sub-continent. At best, it aspires to represent the Hindu people, and to assimilate non-Hindus into its folds by whatever means possible. The Supreme Court has not only effectively condoned this political vision, it has elevated it to a description of an existing state of affairs.[49] It can hardly come as a surprise that the Hindu Right has claimed the decision as an unequivocal victory.[50]

[49] The Court did attempt to distinguish the meaning of the word in the abstract, from the way in which communists and/or fundamentalists may have attempted to *misuse* the word. For instance, the Court stated: 'The mischief resulting from the misuse of the terms by anyone in his speech has to be checked and not its permissible use. It is indeed very unfortunate, if in spite of the liberal and tolerant features of "Hinduism" recognized in judicial decisions, these terms are misused by anyone during the elections to gain any unfair political advantage. Fundamentalism of any colour or kind must be curbed with a heavy hand to preserve and promote the secular creed of the nation', p. 24. In so doing, the Court was attempting to distance itself from the communalist agenda of the Hindu Right, and should not be seen to be *explicitly* endorsing this agenda. Our point, however, is that the term cannot be abstracted from the political and historical context which has given meaning to 'Hindutva'. It is simply not possible to speak of Hindutva as an abstract representation of 'a way of life of the subcontinent', and in so doing, the Court has, perhaps inadvertently, condoned the discursive agenda of the Hindu Right.

[50] We do not mean to suggest that the Court has done so intentionally. In other words, we are not suggesting that the Court has been communalized, and is now simply espousing the views o the Hindu Right. Rather, the flaws in the Supreme Court's reasoning can be seen to lie in the Court's failure to appreciate the political and historical context of the term 'Hindutva', as well as the unstated norms of the majority that are so often reflected in legal decisions.

The efforts of the Supreme Court to clarify its views has allayed the fears of many of those committed to secular democracy.[51] But we remain unpersuaded. In its rejection of the review petition, the Court failed to appreciate precisely where the problems lie. It did not address the highly problematic and unsustainable conclusions about the meaning of Hindutva as a way of life in the subcontinent. The conclusion remains without jurisprudential precedent, and without any appreciation of the historical, political and social context of the term Hindutva. The Court has failed to see how its conclusions on the meaning of the term Hindutva will allow those forces committed to establishing a Hindu Rashtra to continue to pursue their agenda, fearless of the implications of appealing to the concept of Hindutva. In our view, the conclusions of the Court have left the legal framework of the democratic politics considerably weakened against the political use of religion by the Hindu Right. Despite the prohibition on such an appeal in the Representation of the People Act, 1951 and the Supreme Court's emphasis that it has not sanctioned such appeals, the *Manohar Joshi* case has, perhaps unwittingly, given the Hindu Right a green light to continue its Hindutva campaigns and its efforts to establish a Hindu Rashtra. Although strictly speaking, an appeal to Hindutva has not been completely immunized from prosecution under the Act, in so far as the Court has emphasized that it is the *specific context* in which it is used that must be examined, the Court's conclusions on the meaning of Hindutva have nevertheless legitimized the term. The Hindu Right is free to continue its appeal to Hindutva and to the establishment of a Hindu state if it is careful to not too directly

---

[51] See, for example, 'SC: No Misuse of Religion', *Communalism Combat*, 21 (April 1996) p. 4.

appeal to the religion of the candidate,[52] and the Hindu Right has wasted no time in doing just that. Its main electoral platform in the 1996 national elections was once again Hindutva.[53] It appeared again in the 1998 campaign, with the BJP Election Manifesto making considerable mileage out of the Supreme Court decision:

Every effort to characterize Hindutva as a sectarian or exclusive idea has failed as the people of India have repeatedly reflected such a view and the Supreme Court too, finally endorsed the true meaning and content of Hindutva as being consistent with the true meaning and definition of secularism. In fact, Hindutva accepts as sacred all forms of belief and worship. Hindutva means justice for all.[54]

Not only did the Supreme Court decision allow for the continued use of the term Hindutva in electoral politics, but the BJP has used the decision to further legitimize its political use of religion.

The prohibition on the promotion of religious enmity and hatred is also left weakened in the aftermath of the decision. Although the Court did condemn Thackeray for promoting

---

[52] There is also the fact that the Court has established a very strict test for establishing that a candidate has consented to the views of other speakers associated with his/her political party and/or other organization of the Hindu Right. The mere presence of a candidate, on stage with another speaker who appeals to religion or promotes enmity and hatred, is not sufficient proof of that candidate's consent. The implication of this conclusion is that the Hindu Right can carefully orchestrate its rallies, and ensure that the appeals to religion and the promotion of religious enmity come from speakers other than the candidates. The BJP and Shiv Sena will thus be able to continue to reap the benefits of the dirty work done by the RSS and the VHP, and, indeed, even by the non-electoral members/leaders of their own parties. This question of consent is to be heard by the Constitutional Bench of the Supreme Court. 'Constitution Bench will Decide Religion Issue' *Times of India*, Apr 17, 1996.

[53] See 'BJP For a Strong and Prosperous India' Election Manifesto, 1996.

[54] BJP 1998 Election Manifesto, p. 4.

hatred towards the Muslim community, the Court did not recognize the extent to which the concept of Hindutva itself implies an attack on minority rights. While the Court's findings against Thackeray signal that his rhetoric remains beyond the realm of legitimate political speech, it is difficult to imagine speeches more loaded with hatred toward a minority religious group than those of Thackeray.[55] If the prohibition on the promotion of enmity and religious hatred to garner votes is to

[55] Interestingly, even one of the articles in the *Organiser* agreed that in finding Thackeray guilty of a corrupt practice, 'the Court rightly deplored bigotry'. *Organiser*, Dec 24, 1995, p. 3. However, the article continued: 'Bigotry is bad whether it is religious or linguistic, or for that matter casteist. Pseudo-secularists indulging in minorityism and casteists masquerading as messiahs of "social justice" stand exposed before the bar of public opinion. They are guilty of spreading communalism and creating social disharmony.' While condemning Thackeray's speech as bigotry, the *Organiser* article nevertheless used the opportunity to turn the criticism back onto the so-called 'pseudo-secularists', who are alleged to be the real bigots. It is also interesting to note that in the 1996 national election campaign, the BJP distanced itself from some of its more vociferous proponents of hate speech towards Muslims, most notably Uma Bharati and Sadhvi Rithambhara. ('Uma, Sadhvi are not on BJP Bandwagon', *Times of India*, Apr 14, 1996), a shift that was also in keeping with the decision to have the more moderate Vajpayee lead the party, displacing the more militant Advani who had led the party through the Ayodhya campaign. This shift, undoubtedly calculated to maximize their popularity at the polls, has not resolved the more permanent tension within the BJP between its moderate and extreme elements. Despite the condemnation of the shift in the party strategy from within its own ranks, most notably by Uma Bharati, there is ample evidence to suggest that the BJP retains its commitment to undermining minority rights. For instance, one of the election advertisements of the BJP (significantly with Advani's picture, not Vajpayee's) continued the attack on Muslim minorities under the traditional slogan 'Justice for All, Appeasement for None'.

The shift may simply have been an effort to be somewhat more careful during the 1996 election, and again in the 1998 election campaign, of not violating the prohibition on the promotion of religious enmity, and part of its bid for political power, by trying to attract voters who were disillusioned

mean anything at all, it would have to encapsulate such speech.[56] At the same time, the more technical aspects of the Supreme Court decisions have created ample opportunity for the Hindu Right to continue its often vehement attacks on minorities. The narrow test established by the Court for proving that a candidate consented to the speeches of another allows the Hindu Right to carefully orchestrate its campaigns, ensuring that speakers other than electoral candidates are assigned the task of spewing the most hateful rhetoric.[57] Moreover, as we discuss in the next section, the Court's conclusions on the secular nature of some of the speeches of the Hindu Right will continue to allow considerable latitude to electoral candidates to attack the legitimacy of minority rights, provided that the attack is adequately disguised within the discourse of secularism and equality.

---

with the Congress, and then United Front governments, but uncomfortable with the more militant face of the party. Although it is still (at the time of writing) Vajpayee who is Prime Minister, Advani occupies the very powerful position of Home Minister. The difference in their rhetoric continues to be striking. Despite the fact that the BJP was forced to abandon part of its Hindutva platform in its National Agenda for Governance with its coalition partners, Advani's rhetoric continues very much along the line of the Hindu Right's more extreme cultural nationalism.

[56] There is increasingly a question of whether the laws directed at prohibiting hate speech can mean anything at all, with the increasing legitimacy being accorded to the speech of the Hindu Right. As the speech of the Hindu Right becomes more mainstream, and more part of the collective common sense of an increasing number of Hindu subjects, the efficacy of the hate speech provisions, intended only to police the margins of intolerable speech, is undermined. For a more detailed discussion of this problem, see Kapur, chapter 1, n. 10.

[57] See Basu et al., chapter 1, n. 2.

4

Vindicating 'Pseudo-secularism'

...when Hinduism is no religion and is a way of life, to say that a Hindu state is anti-secular is wholly incorrect... Hinduism is secularism par excellence.

Organiser, Jan 21, 1996, p. 2

The failure of the Court to appreciate the meaning of Hindutva, and thus, the implications of its deployment in the political landscape has done an enormous disservice to the cause of secularism. But the extent of the damage does not end here. Rather, the damage has in our view been compounded by the Court's comments on the secular nature of some of the speeches of the BJP candidates. In this section, we begin by briefly reviewing these comments, and then attempt to illustrate their dangerous implications by situating these comments within the broader context of the highly contested meaning of secularism, and the efforts of the Hindu Right to appropriate secularism for its own rather non-secular purposes. Finally, we challenge the views of the Supreme Court that there is nothing inconsistent between its conclusions, and earlier decisions of the Constitutional Bench of the Supreme Court on secularism, particularly, *Bommai*.[1]

SIMPLY SECULAR?

In considering whether an appeal to Hindutva constituted a violation of the Representation of the People Act, 1951, the Court took into account the fact that many of the Hindu Right speeches at issue appealed to the principle of secularism, and to violations of the right to equality. In the Court's view:

It cannot be doubted that a speech with a secular stance alleging discrimination against any particular religion and promising removal of the imbalance cannot be treated as an appeal on the ground of religion as its thrust is for promoting secularism. Instances given in the speech of discrimination against any religion causing the imbalance in the professed goal of secularism, the allegation being against any individual or any political party, cannot be called an appeal on the ground of religion forbidden by sub-section (3). In other words, mention of religion as such in an election speech is not forbidden by sub-section (3) so long as it does not amount to an appeal to vote for a candidate on the ground of his religion or to refrain from voting for any other candidate on the ground of his religion.[2]

According to the Court, any election speech 'made in conformity with the fundamental right to freedom of religion guaranteed under Articles 25 to 30 of the Constitution cannot be treated as anti-secular to be prohibited by sub-section (3) of Section 123, unless it falls within the narrow net of the prohibitions.'[3] A speech that refers to 'religion during an election

---

[1] See chapter 1, n. 13.

[2] Prabhoo, chapter 2, n. 1, p. 1123 para 16.

[3] Ibid., para 18.

campaign with a secular stance in conformity with the fundamental right to freedom of religion' is outside the purview of
section 123(3) unless it includes an appeal to vote for or against
a candidate on the basis of his religion. Similarly, in *Ramakant
Mayekar*, the Court stated: 'There can be no doubt that mention
of any religion in the context of secularism of [sic] for criticizing
the anti-secular stance of any political party or candidate cannot
amount to a corrupt practice.'[4] The subtext of these comments
is quite clear: the fact that the candidates were criticizing the
'pseudo-secularism' of the Congress Government and pointing
out the discrimination against Hindus within this version of
secularism, meant that the speech was of a secular nature.

In our view, these small passages represent some of the most
insidious dimensions of the inroads made by the Hindu Right.
In this passage, the Supreme Court has effectively legitimized
the secular nature of the Hindu Right's version of secularism.
The paradox of the Hindu Right's version of secularism has
entered officially into legal discourse. Their long struggle to
popularize and legitimize a version of secularism that effectively
undermines all prevailing notions of secularism has won yet
another important ideological victory, in having been awarded
a judicial seal of approval. In order to illustrate the dangerous
implications of these passages, we first briefly review the
dominant discourse of secularism within constitutional law, and
the way in which the Hindu Right has appropriated this
discourse for its own (non-secular) purposes.

CONTESTING SECULARISMS

Although generally considered to be a cornerstone of Indian
democracy, secularism has long been a highly contested concept

---

[4] *Ramakant Mayekar*, chapter 2, n. 1, p. 834 para 27.

in India.[5] From the days of the independence struggle, two very different understandings of secularism have competed for ideological dominance. Jawaharlal Nehru, the first Prime Minister of independent India, had a vision of secularism—described as *dharma nirapeksata*—which was based on a strong belief in the need to separate religion and politics.[6] By way of contrast, Mahatma Gandhi's vision—*sarva dharma samabhava*—rejected the idea of the separation of religion and politics, and was based instead on the principle of equal respect for all religions. The contest between these two visions of secularism can be seen within the broader context of western conceptualizations of secularism, and debates regarding its appropriateness within the Indian context. The liberal democratic vision of secularism is generally seen as characterized by three principles: (1) liberty and freedom of religion; (2) citizenship, and the right to equality and non-discrimination; and (3) neutrality, and the separation of state and religion.[7] The first two principles have posed little controversy in the Indian context. Rather, the right to freedom of religion and the right to equality and non-discrimination, are generally recognized as important constitutional values in their

[5] K. T. Shah, a member of the Constituent Assembly, attempted on two separate occasions to have the term included in the Constitution, but was not successful. In 1973, the Supreme Court held that secularism was a part of the basic foundation and structure of the Constitution, in the case of *Kesavananda Bharati v. State of Kerala* AIR 1973 SC 1461. It was only in 1976 that the term 'secularism' was inserted into the Constitution with the 42nd Amendment.

[6] This conceptualization of secularism was seen most clearly in the Karachi Resolution of the Congress on Fundamental Rights (1931), which provided: 'the state shall observe neutrality in regard to all religions'. As many commentators have observed, however, Nehru eventually compromised on his vision of secularism, and adopted the concept of equal respect for all religions. For a discussion see Asgar Ali Engineer, 'Secularism in India: Theory and Practice', in *Secularism and Liberation*, p. 40.

[7] See generally, Donald Eugene Smith, *India as a Secular State* (1964).

own right as well as a foundation of Indian secularism.[8] The problem arises, however, in relation to the third principle, that is, of the separation of religion and state. It is in regard to this third principle that some commentators have argued that India is not a secular state;[9] and others have argued that India has some but not all of the features of a secular state;[10] and that yet others argue that if India is to be a secular state, it must develop its own distinctive understanding of the requirements of secularism. It is in relation to this third principle that the Nehruvian and Gandhian models part company. Nehru was committed to a separation of religion and politics, whereas Gandhi was of the view that such a separation was neither possible nor desirable within the Indian context. Rather, a distinctively Indian conceptualization of secularism was required; a secularism which would be more in keeping with the culture and tradition of the Indian people. *Sarva dharma samabhava* was in Gandhi's view, such a vision. It is this understanding of secularism as equal respect for all religions that has come to dominate legal and political thought.[11]

[8] There has, however, been considerable criticism of the extent to which the Indian constitutional and political framework has upheld these values. See for example, Smith, Ibid., who was critical of the extent to which these principles were compromised in the Constitution, which allowed for state intervention in the affairs of religion.

[9] See V. P. Luthra, *The Concept of Secular State and India* (1964).

[10] See Smith above n. 7.

[11] The argument that secularism in India does not mean a wall of separation between religion and politics, but rather, the equal respect for all religions is common throughout the legal literature. For a typical example, see Engineer, above n. 6, who argues that the western concept of secularism, which involves indifference to religion, has never taken root in India. 'The concept of secularism in India emerged, in the context of religious pluralism as against religious authoritarianism in the west... It was religious community, rather than religious authority, which mattered in the Indian context.' At the same time, it is important to recognize that this dominant concept of secularism

Within the context of constitutional law and discourse, discussions of secularism typically focus on the right to freedom of religion and the right to equality, the first two of the general principles of liberal democratic vision of secularism. The literature typically highlights the various provisions of the Constitution that are considered relevant to the principle of equal respect for all religions: Articles 14 and 15, guaranteeing the right to equality and non-discrimination; and Articles 25–6 guaranteeing the right to freedom of religion and the right of religious denominations to organize their own affairs. The right to equality and the right to freedom of religion are, within this vision, seen as fundamentally interconnected, that is, that all citizens must have the *equal* right to freedom of religion, and that the State must not *discriminate* on the basis of religion. Following from the dominant understanding of secularism as *sarva dharma samabhava*, the constitutional discourse does not insist on a wall of separation between religion and politics.[12] Rather discussions tend to emphasize the principle of toleration,

---

is a contested one, which many critics have questioned, challenged and rejected. We discuss these challenges further below in the section entitled 'Secularism in Crisis'.

[12] See, for example, P. B. Gajendragadkar, 'Secularism: Its Implications for Law and Life in India', in G. S. Sharma (ed.), *Secularism: Its Implications For Law And Life In India*, (1966). 'The State does not owe loyalty to any one particular religion as such; it is not irreligious or anti-religion; it gives equal freedom for all religions and holds that the religion of the citizen has nothing to do in the matter of socio-economic problems'; R. L.Chaudhari, *The Concept Of Secularism In Indian Constitution* (1987) who writes 'the absence of complete separation between the state and the religion is because of the character of Indian society which is basically religious... Separation of the state from the religion is not the basis of Indian secularism, as it is in other countries. Indian Constitution does not reject religion. On the contrary, it respects all religions'. See also J. M. Shelat, *Secularism: Principles and Applications* (1972), pp 121–2.

that is, of equal toleration for all religions.[13] In this regard, Article 51A prohibiting the establishment of a state religion is generally highlighted, as are the constitutional prohibitions on religious instruction in state schools, and on taxation in support

[13] See, for example, the work of P. K. Tripathi, 'Secularism, Law and the Constitution of India', in *Secularism In India* (1966), who articulated three basic principles of Indian secularism: (1) the principle of the primacy of the individual, who is placed above and before religion; (2) the principle of freedom of religion and religious denomination; and (3) the principle of toleration. Neutrality is thus replaced with an emphasis on toleration. See also, P. K. Tripathi, 'Secularism: Constitutional Provision and Judicial Review', in *Secularism: Its Implications For Law And Life In India*, ibid., p. 165. See also, Upendra Baxi, 'The Struggle for the Redefinition of Secularism in India: Some Preliminary Reflections', in *Secularism and Liberation*, chapter 3, n. 18, who argues that these principles find recognition in the Indian constitution. Baxi identifies several other features of Indian secularism that have been affirmed through constitutional decisions: (i) the state by itself, shall not espouse or establish or practice any religion; (ii) public revenues will not be used to promote any religion; (iii) the state shall have the power to regulate any 'economic, financial or other secular activity' associated with religious practice (Article 25(2)(a) of the Constitution); (iv) the state shall have the power through the law to provide for 'social welfare and reform or the throwing open of Hindu religious institutions of public character to all classes and sections of Hindus' (Article 25(2)(b) of the Constitution); (v) the practice of untouchability is constitutionally outlawed by Article 17; (vi) every individual person will have, in that order, an equal right to freedom of conscience and religion; (viii) these rights are furthermore subject to other fundamental rights in Part III; (ix) the Courts, especially the Supreme Court, shall have the final 'say' on adjudging state action as valid or otherwise under the above principles. See *Kesavananda Bharati* and *Indira Gandhi* cases. Another feature was added through a constitutional amendment which imposed a fundamental duty on all citizens to 'preserve the rich heritage of our composite culture'. (Article 51-A(f)). Baxi places considerable reliance on the Courts and judiciary in determining the meaning of secularism in India and argues that such a constitutional perspective has been absent from public debate. He argues that the judiciary can bring a sharper focus to the debate. While we agree that the judiciary has a role to play, the Hindutva decision highlights how the judiciary has failed to so do.

of any particular religion. The constitutional guarantees on equality and freedom of religion which are seen to frame this principle of equal toleration are also again highlighted. The constitutional characterization of secularism can, then, be seen to be characterized by three principles: (1) freedom of religion, (2) equality and non-discrimination and (3) toleration. Toleration thus comes to displace neutrality as the third principle of secularism.[14] It is this subtle but important shift from neutrality to toleration that captures the essence of the *sarva dharma samabhava* vision of secularism, and its conceptualization of the appropriate relationship between religion and state. In stark contrast to the western liberal democratic model, which insists that the relationship must be characterized by non-intervention, the 'equal respect for all religions' model allows for state intervention in religion, provided that such intervention is in accordance with the requirements of equality and freedom of religion.[15]

Within this constitutional framework, there is, then, a general sense that state intervention in religion is not prohibited. There is also a general sense that equality is intricately connected to secularism: equal respect for all religions requires that all individuals and religious communities have the equal right to

[14] Although there are some echoes of the principle of neutrality within the constitutional discourse, these discussions tend to infuse the concept of neutrality with the spirit of *sarva dharma samabhava*. Neutrality to all religions tends not to be associated with a wall of separation, as it is in the American context, but rather with the idea that the State must not discriminate against any religion.

[15] Smith, n. 7 above, has argued that the third principle of liberal democratic secularism regarding the separation of religion and state includes two distinct principles: '(1) the non-interference of the state and religious organizations in each other's affairs; (2) the absence of a legal connection between the state and a particular religion. The Indian Constitution...does not subscribe to the first principle; it does however uphold the second' (p. 133).

freedom of religion (to practise, profess, and propagate their religion), and that the State does not discriminate among citizens on the basis of their religion. But the more specific question of the kind of state action mandated by this vision of secularism remains unanswered. What kind of state action is required to ensure that all individuals and communities have an equal right to freedom of religion? What kind of state action is required to ensure that no citizen is discriminated against on the basis of his or her religion? Although this vision of secularism allows some form of state intervention, in so far as it does not require the wall of separation between state and religion, the *kind* of intervention mandated by this vision of secularism remains undefined. Does equal respect for all religions require that the Government treat all religions the same? Or does this principle require that the Government equally accommodate different religions? There is nothing on the face of the concept itself that resolves this question.[16]

[16] Some have suggested that it requires that the State treat all religions in a *neutral* and impartial manner. But the requirement of neutrality does little to clarify the precise meaning of secularism. Does neutrality require that the State stay out of the affairs of the religious communities? Such an understanding begins to sound rather like the doctrine of separation of religion and politics, which this model explicitly rejects. Alternatively, then, would neutrality require that the State treat religious communities the same way? Or is the State acting neutrally when it treats religious communities in a way that ensures an equal result? This question has been an ongoing dilemma within the context of American constitutional law, and the anti-establishment clause of the First Amendment. Many have argued that facial neutrality is often premised on and serves to reinforce the unstated norms of the majority. Martha Minow has argued for example that facial neutrality of the clause ignores and risks reinforcing its non-neutral impact. Martha Minow, 'Supreme Court, 1986 Term, Foreword: Justice Engendered', *Harvard Law Review* 10 (1987), p. 22. See also Minow, *Making All The Difference: Inclusion, Exclusion and American Law* (1990), p. 44. This critique of neutrality in the American context is discussed further below in the section on 'Secularism in Crisis'. For

As we have argued elsewhere, the debate over the meaning of secularism is very much a debate over the meaning of equality, and as such much of the confusion over the meaning of secularism derives from the confusion over that of equality.[17] Any attempt to resolve the meaning of secularism requires a shift in attention to the meaning of equality—a concept that is no less contested within the contemporary Indian polity. The dominant understanding of equality in India, particularly within the context of constitutional law, has been one of formal equality, that is, on formally equal treatment.[18] But a second approach to equality is also discernible in Indian political and legal thought, that is, one of substantive or compensatory equality. In this understanding, equality is concerned not with equal treatment, but with addressing disadvantage. Substantive equality, as we have elaborated in our work, is directed at eliminating the historic and systemic discrimination against disadvantaged groups that operates to undermine their full and equal participation in social, economic, political and cultural life.[19] In the Indian context, this approach to equality is often referred to as 'compensatory discrimination', which is intended to capture the idea that certain individuals or groups may need to be treated differently in order to compensate for the

---

the moment, it is sufficient to note that the emphasis on neutrality thus does little to clarify the precise meaning of equal respect for all religions. Moreover, because of its echoes with a wall of separation approach, the criteria of neutrality may only further obscure the meaning of this vision of secularism.

[17] See Kapur and Cossman, Introduction, n. 1 (1993).

[18] For a detailed discussion of these competing visions of equality in the context of Indian constitutional law, see Ratna Kapur and Brenda Cossman, 'On Women, Equality and the Constitution: Through the Looking Glass of Feminism', *National Law School Journal*, Special Edition, Feminism and Law, (1993); also, Kapur and Cossman, *Subversive Sites*, Introduction, n. 1.

[19] Ibid.

discrimination they have suffered. These very different under-standings of equality have very different implications for secularism. A formal understanding of equality would insist that the government treat all religions the same. A substantive understanding of equality, on the other hand, would require that the government accommodate religious differences, particu-larly those of minority religious groups, which have suffered from historic and systemic disadvantage.

There has, however, been surprisingly little attention to this question of the meaning of equality within the dominant vision of secularism. This continuing silence on the underlying con-ception of equality is no longer a harmless oversight. As we illustrate in the next section, it has become a dangerous silence that the Hindu Right has been only too willing to exploit in its quest to claim the terrain of secularism as its own. The discursive strategies of the Hindu Right have been based on bringing a very particular understanding of equality to the popular understanding of secularism, with powerful results.

In the Name of Secularism

The Hindu Right has staked its claim to secularism, casting itself as the only true upholder of Indian secularism. Increasingly, as this claim comes to have more and more popular appeal, it is an appeal that those dedicated to the cause of secular democracy can no longer afford to ignore. As we have argued elsewhere, a more detailed examination of the strategy of the Hindu Right reveals how skilfully it has deployed constitutional discourses of secularism and equality.[20] The parties of Hindu Right have appropriated the concept of secularism and through various spurious yet ingenious discursive moves, made it very much their own. Secularism has now become the official banner under

[20] See Kapur and Cossman, 1993, Introduction, n. 1.

which the Hindu Right campaigns for a Hindu Rashtra, and under which the rights of religious minorities are being savagely attacked and delegitimized.[21] Moreover, its claim to secularism is intricately connected to its understanding of equality.

[21] It is perhaps worth noting, however, that there is also a weak dissenting voice within the Hindu Right that argues against the principle of secularism. For instance, several recent opinion articles can be found in the *Organiser* arguing against secularism. In 'The Anti-Secular Syndrome', *Organiser* Mar 8, 1998, Anand Shankar Pandya, after making the typical 'pseudo secularism' attacks on the enemies of the Hindu Right, and the view that for Hindus, secularism is spiritual rather than political, then argues: 'India's true ideals were consigned to the dustbin long back, when the powers that be replaced them with alien concepts of socialism and secularism. Those inimical ideologies have undermined our traditional wisdom and harmed the nation. In fact, secularism is against the tenets of the Gita, wherein Lord Krishna·says he would appear on this earth to rescue dharma whenever it is in danger', *Organiser*, p. 2. M. V. Kamath in 'Facing Up to History', Feb 15, 1998, writes: 'For the Hindu self-renewal is an impossibility under the deadening hold of the secular ideology. That ideology had to be discarded lock, stock and barrel, and the process has begun... One cannot renew Hinduism if one does not accept its reality. In consequence, secularism has had to be sacrificed... Once India is liberated from the secular bonds that are presently tying it down to earth there is no knowing to what heights of glory it can rise', p. 6. And again, in 'Secular Stigma Must be Removed', *Organiser* June 7, 1998, Dr Abraham Varghese argues that secularism as a concept is not necessary for India, since a respect for religions is deeply rooted in Indian tradition. He writes 'The concept of secularism is the last wedge driven by the departing colonial power into the Indian society to make it perpetually divided. In fact there is no need for the term "secular" to appear in the Constitution or dominate all our political parties. It is high time we removed this stigma and colonial stamp from our national identity', p. 2. These writers argue that the very concept of secularism should be rejected, although they do so from very different perspectives. While the first two base their argument quite explicitly on religion, the third appears to base his argument more on an anti-colonial political rhetoric. We do not want to make too much of these lone voices arguing against secularism, since the official position of the BJP and the RSS continues to be one of secularism. However, their continued appearance is at least noteworthy.

The Hindu Right has explicitly argued in favour of *sarva dharma samabhava* and 'positive secularism'. The BJP has repeatedly stated its support for this version of secularism. For instance, the BJP Constitution provides 'The Party shall be committed to ...Positive Secularism, that is, *sarva dharma samabhava*'.[22] The 1990 BJP Manifesto similarly stated: 'The BJP believes in positive secularism which, according to our constitution makers, meant *sarva dharma samabhava* and which does not connote an irreligious state.'[23] Along the way, there appears to have been a small shift in their discourse. While the BJP continues to speak of 'positive secularism', it now uses the term *sarva panth samadara*, which it translates as 'the equal respect for all faiths'.[24] The discourse of secularism is based on a particular vision of equal respect for all faiths, that is, on formally equal treatment. Within this view, the equality of all religions requires that all religious communities be treated the

[22] Article IV, BJP Constitution and Rules, as approved by the National Council May 2, 1992.

[23] See BJP Manifesto as quoted in speech delivered by L. K. Advani, in parliament on November 7, 1990. Interestingly, the 1996 BJP Election Manifesto did not mention secularism at all. But, in his prime ministerial address to the nation, Atal Bihari Vajpayee spoke of the BJP's secular vision, and emphasized that under the BJP, India would never be a theocratic state.

[24] See 1998 BJP Election Manifesto, p. 36. This language also appears in the BJP and Alliance Partner's National Agenda for Governance, 1998, p. 7. This reference to *sarva panth samadar* also appeared in A. B. Vajpayee's address to the nation when he was very briefly sworn in as India's Prime Minister in 1996. We have as yet been unable to account for this small shift in their discourse on secularism, or to determine what significance, if any, is to be attached to this shift from the equal respect for all *religions*, to the equal respect for all *faiths*. One suggestion is that the word 'Panth' has replaced the word 'Dharma' as a way of further legitimizing the secular credentials of the Hindu Right, in so far as 'Panth' is somewhat less associated with the Hindu religion than is the word 'Dharma'. We are, however, unable to confirm this suggestion.

same in law. For example, L. K. Advani states: 'The BJP is committed unequivocally to secularism as conceived by our Constitution makers. All citizens are equal and there shall be no discrimination between one citizen and another, on grounds of his faith'.[25] Similarly, as the BJP 1998 election manifesto declared: 'The BJP's concept of positive secularism is Justice for All, Appeasement for None'.[26] Any special or different treatment, on the basis of religion, is seen as a violation of secularism. The same emphasis on formally equal treatment can be seen in RSS political rhetoric: 'The RSS...never demands any special rights to the Hindus. At the same time, it is against giving any concession to other religious minority groups and it opposes religious discrimination.'[27]

The particular meaning that the Hindu Right gives to the equal respect for all religions is one based on formally equal treatment. Accordingly, any laws or policies that provide special treatment for minorities are opposed as 'pseudo-secularism', or

[25] L. K. Advani, Press Conference, Jan 18, 1993. Similar statements can be found in articles and commentaries throughout *Organiser*. For example, Madhok writes: 'There are three universally accepted essential postulates of a secular state: 1. The state must not discriminate between its citizens on the basis of religion or form of worship. 2. There should be uniform laws for all citizens. 3. All citizens should be equal before the law', Balraj Madhok 'An Open Letter to the President, Prime Minister, Party Leaders and Editors', *Organiser*, Republic Day 1993 Nationalism Special, p. 52. Precisely the same formulation is restated by Madhok more recently in 'The National Agenda', *Organiser*, Feb 1, 1998, p. 11. Within this definition, secularism is rendered synonymous with the formally equal treatment of all citizens. Significantly, there is no mention of a non-denominational state within this definition of secularism. Nor is there any reference to the principles of freedom of religion and toleration.

[26] 1998 BJP Election Manifesto, p. 36.

[27] K. Jayaprasad, *RSS and Hindu Nationalism* (1991) p. 93. See also Nana Deshmukh, *RSS: Victim of Slander* (1979).

the 'appeasement of minorities.' In the discursive strategy of the Hindu Right, this approach to secularism is made to sound quite reasonable. It has been based on the *sarva dharma samabhava* approach to secularism, which is after all the quintessential understanding of secularism in India, and the formal approach to equality, which has been the dominant understanding of equality within Indian constitutional law.[28] Beneath the surface, however, this discourse of secularism and equality is an unapologetic appeal to brute majoritarianism and an assault on the very legitimacy of minority rights.[29] The formal equality of the Hindu Right means that the dominant Hindu community becomes the norm against which all other communities are to be judged and the norm according to which these 'other' communities are to be treated. In the hands of the Hindu Right, not only is special protection for the rights of minorities rejected as a violation of secularism, but moreover, their leaders defend this vision of secularism in unapologetically majoritarianist terms. For example, Seshadri writes:

Democracy in normal parlance means the rule of the majority. In every single democratic country, it is the majority culture whose ideals and values of life are accepted as the national ethos by one and

[28] Although as mentioned, the BJP has shifted its discourse from *sarva dharma samabhava* to *sarva panth samadara* in its most recent manifesto, the BJP's own translation of the new term as the equal respect for all faiths appears to continue to be based on the Gandhian tradition of equal respect for all religions. In the National Agenda for Governance, 1998, for example, the BJP with its partners writes: 'We will truly and genuinely uphold and practise *the concept of secularism consistent with the Indian tradition* of *sarva panth samadara* (equal respect for all faiths) and on the basis of equality for all.' (emphasis added), p. 7. The BJP is thus still claiming that its conception of secularism is consistent with the traditional conception of Indian secularism.

[29] For a discussion of the dangers of majoritarianism that lie within this vision of secularism, see P. C. Upadhyaya, 'The Politics of Indian Secularism', *Modern Asian Studies*, 26:4 (1992), p. 815.

all...The same applies to the laws of the land...No religious group can claim any exclusive rights or privileges to itself.[30]

One of the very cornerstones of democracy—the protection of minorities from the rule of the majority—is simply discarded Through this approach, the Hindu Right is attempting to establish majority norms as the ostensibly neutral norms against which all others are judged. Their norm is a Hindu norm. According to their vision, the role of the State in religion is thus not one of neutrality at all, but of fostering the Hindu nation. We can see the paradox of this vision of secularism carried to its contradictory extreme. The practices of the Hindu majority come to be viewed as neutral, and the State in turn is seen to be acting neutrally only when it reinforces these practices. Thus, Hindus do not need 'special rights' because of the extent to which all legal rights come to be based on Hindu cultural norms and practices. The discourse of secularism comes to reinforce the norms of the dominant Hindu community.

The reconstruction of secularism within the political rhetoric of the Hindu Right has also relied on the principle of toleration; a principle which, in the hands of the Hindu Right, is cast in wholly religious terms. Golwalkar, speaking on the question of secularism, stated:

It sometimes seems to mean a denial of all religion—and carries a connotation of being materialistic...But if by secularism is meant that the State should not be tagged to any particular creed and that all faiths should be equally respected, then this again would be another name of Hindu tradition. In fact, Hindu tradition goes far beyond the western concept of 'tolerance' which implies that the faith which 'tolerates' is superior to the other. With us, all faiths are equally sacred...Hinduism is secularism in its noblest sense.[31]

[30] H. V. Seshadri, 'Strange Political Diction', *Organiser*, Feb 4, 1990.

[31] M. S. Golwalkar, 'From Red Fort Grounds', speech delivered at a public rally at the Red Fort Grounds, Nov 14, 1965, (transcript available at the Nehru Memorial Museum and Library).

Echoing the views of the ideological leaders of the Hindu Right before him, Deoras of the RSS, similarly argues that only Hindus are capable of real secularism:

If secularism means treating all religions on an equal footing, proselytisation and secularism can't go together. Those who believe in conversion do so because they feel that their religion is superior to all others. Their organizations therefore cannot claim to be secular. Hinduism, on the other hand, does not believe in conversions and Hindus have never been proselytisers. As such, organizations of Hindus alone can be truly secular.[32]

Secularism is defined as the toleration of all religions. Hinduism is defined as the only religion with a true tolerance for all other religions. Therefore, according to these terms, only a country based on Hinduism can be truly secular. The norm of the dominant Hindu community, which remains unstated in the Hindu Right's political rhetoric around equality and non-discrimination is here stated quite explicitly: 'Hinduism is secularism par excellence'.[33] And paradoxically, it is precisely this argument that is used to deflect any allegation of fundamentalism or theocracy. Because Hinduism is tolerant, because it represents 'secularism par excellence', by definition, it cannot be fundamentalist or theocratic.

Revealingly, there is little emphasis on the second principle of Indian secularism, namely freedom of religion, within the Hindu Right. For example, neither the BJPs Constitution nor its manifestos explicitly refer to freedom of religion as a basic commitment. There is a reference within its Constitution to 'liberty of faith' as a basic objective, but the term is not synonymous with the constitutional guarantees of freedom of religion. Rather, when the idea of 'liberty of faith' is raised, it

[32] Balasaheb Deoras, *Answers Questions* (1984), p. 53.
[33] *Organiser*, Jan 21, 1996, p. 2.

tends to be subsumed within the more general rubric of toleration, and is used to distinguish Hindu Rashtra from a theocratic state. For instance, in *Integral Humanism*, Deendayal Upadhyaya emphasized that Dharma Rajya[34] 'does not mean a theocratic state...Where a particular sect and its prophet or Guru rule supreme, that is a theocratic state. All the rights are enjoyed by the followers of this particular sect. Others either cannot live in that country or at best enjoin a slave-like, secondary citizen's status'.[35] Upadhyaya insisted that such was not to be the case in Dharma Rajya:

In a theocratic state one religion has all the rights and advantages, and there are direct or indirect restrictions on all other religions. Dharma Rayja accepts the importance of religion in the peace, happiness and progress of an individual. Therefore the state has the responsibility to maintain an atmosphere in which every individual can follow the religion of his choice and live in peace. *The freedom to follow one's own religion necessarily requires tolerance for other religions.*[36] [emphasis added]

But the freedom of religion within this vision is a highly restricted one. First, the idea of 'liberty of faith' or 'freedom to worship' is cast in highly individualistic terms: it is the individual's right to pursue his or her own spiritual path; it is not the collective rights of a religious community to any form of self-determination. Rather, these collective rights, such as the right to set up educational institutions as guaranteed by

[34] The term 'Dharma Rajya' used by Upadhyaya and taken up by the Jana Sangh, and subsequently, by the BJP, can be seen to be a rough equivalent of Hindu Rashtra, a term that has since been explicitly adopted by the BJP.
[35] Deendayal Upadhyaya, *Integral Humanism* (1965), pp 53–4. This text is considered to be the ideological foundation of the BJP, and the term 'integral humanism' has been included in the Party's constitution and policy statements since its inception.
[36] Ibid.

Article 30 of the Constitution, are cast as a violation of equality.[37] Secondly, it is a freedom of religion that is brought under the rubric of Hinduism, that is, Hinduism alone is seen to provide the toleration that is required for individuals to be able to pursue their own spiritual path. The idea of Hinduism as tolerant is again used to prop up the claim to secularism, while framing this claim within an entirely religious discourse. Thirdly, it is a freedom that does not include the right to propagate one's religion. Rather, the propagation of religion is cast as a violation of toleration; as the inability of some religions to tolerate others.[38] More specifically, Islam and Christianity, the proselytizing religions, are seen to be premised upon the non-toleration of other religions, and thus, on the very denial of the right to freedom of religion for those who do not subscribe to their religions. The right to propagate one's religion is thereby transformed from an integral part of freedom of religion into its violation.

The sphere of freedom of religion is thus radically curtailed within the discourse of the Hindu Right. It is contained, on one

[37] The 1998 Election Manifesto, above, n. 26, states, 'Amend Article 30 of the Constitution suitably to remove any scope of discrimination against any religious community in matters of education' (p. 36). The 1996 BJP Election Manifesto, chapter 3, n. 53, had similarly included a commitment to amending Article 30, although as in the 1998 version, it did not specify the particular nature of the amendment. The Manifesto stated that the BJP is committed to 'Ensure equality for all and discrimination against none on the grounds of religion in matters of education by amending Article 30' (p. 64).

[38] Conversions from Hinduism to either Islam or Christianity have long been a major theme within the Hindu Right. Savarkar, Golwalkar, as well as the contemporary ideologues such as Seshadri and Deoras have focused attacks on the proselytizing religions, the problem of conversions, and the goal of bringing those who have strayed from Hinduism back into its fold. Similarly, the *Organiser* is filled with articles dealing with the problem of conversions, detailing recent conversions of Hindus to other religions, and condemning these proselytizing religions for their intolerance.

side, by a formal understanding of equality, which condemns any special treatment to religious minorities as a violation of secularism. On the other side, freedom of religion is contained by a religious understanding of toleration, within which Hinduism becomes the only guarantor of an individual's ability to follow their own religion, and therefore the only guarantor of secularism. Thus framed, the Hindu Right can retain just enough of the discourse of freedom of religion (or liberty of worship) to maintain its claim to secularism, and to distinguish itself from religious fundamentalism.

Through these various manipulations and redefinitions, the Hindu Right is thereby able to cast its arguments within the requirements of the constitutional discourse of secularism. It appeals to the constitutional guarantees of equality in Articles 14 and 15, which in its hands, means the equal treatment of all individuals and communities. It appeals to the principle of toleration, which in its hands, means the supremacy of Hinduism. And it appeals to the constitutional guarantees of freedom of religion in Article 25, which in its hands, means only the individual's right to worship, and is used to reinforce the importance of Hinduism's toleration. Each dimension is carefully deployed to reinforce the other, and to immunize itself from the allegation of religious fundamentalism.

Despite its appearance, the Hindu Right's discourse of 'secularism' fails to conform to any of the prevailing definitions of secularism. It does not, of course, follow the formal approach to secularism in so far as there is no separation of religion and politics. Nor does it in fact follow the *sarva dharma samabhava* approach in so far as there is no real respect or accommodation for any other religion. The Hindu Right does *not* equally respect all religions: since not all religions are as tolerant as Hinduism, then, not all religions are worthy of equal respect. Rather, the objective of Hindutva is the assimilation of minorities into the broader and ostensibly more tolerant fabric of Hinduism. But, increasingly, this version of secularism is capturing the hearts and minds of Hindu subjects, and passing as a reasonable alternative to the other failed versions.

In the *Manohar Joshi* decision, even the Supreme Court has now recognized the Hindu Right's appropriation of the concept of secularism as a reasonable alternative. In the Court's view, speeches that allege discrimination against a religious community are simply part and parcel of the constitutional guarantees of equality and freedom of religion. There is a certain logic to this reasoning, following from the constitutional discourse of secularism: the Hindu Right is appealing to the concept of secularism, and criticizing the failure of the Central Government to implement it. It is casting its arguments in the language of equality—formal equality and discrimination against Hindus. Appeals are expressly made to the guarantees of equality in Articles 14 and 15 of the Constitution. Since the BJP's arguments are thus cast in the discourse of Indian constitutionalism, these arguments are not seen to be an appeal to religion. It is precisely this appeal to the language of secularism and equality that has made the strategies of the Hindu Right so brilliant, and so disturbingly successful. At face value, there is nothing in the constitutional discourse of secularism that seems to prevent it. The Hindu Right is able to take up the concept of equal respect for all religions, and its underlying principles of equality and non-discrimination, freedom of religion and toleration, to argue in favour of a Hindu State. The fact that this constitutional discourse has never insisted on the separation of religion and state, leaves the Hindu Right free to argue for a Hindu Rashtra; the fact that the meaning of equality that ought to inform this vision of secularism has not been clearly articulated, leaves the

Hindu Right free to argue for its vision of equality; and the fact that the constitutional discourse has accepted the importance of toleration of other religions as the essence of Indian secularism, means that the Hindu Right is free to argue that Hinduism alone provides the basis for a tolerant, secular State.

On the one hand, the Supreme Court can simply be seen as having been guided by the basic dictates of constitutional secularism, and seeing the way in which the BJP appealed to this constitutional discourse, rightly concluded that there was no violation of secularism. On the other hand, if constitutional secularism is to be guarded and protected by the judiciary, we might reasonably expect the courts to take a harder look at the claims before it, to look beneath the surface of these claims, and interrogate whether they are in fact consistent with the principles of constitutional secularism. We might, quite reasonably, expect the Court to do so *before* it condones the claims of the Hindu Right to secularism. But, in the *Manohar Joshi* case, such reasonable expectations were not met. Rather, the Court was content to conclude that the speeches were secular simply by virtue of their appeal to the discourse of equality. The Court has, in effect, fallen into the complex discursive trap set by the Hindu Right, wherein a fundamentally non-secular project is being packaged, sold and consumed as a secular one, and in so doing, the Court has, perhaps inadvertently, legitimized this version of secularism with a judicial seal of approval.

It is precisely in this legitimation of the Hindu Right's vision of secularism that the Supreme Court decision has such dangerous implications. The strategy of dressing up its attack on minority rights, and its effort to establish a denominational state in the language of secularism, has become enough to legitimize the Hindu Right's political agenda as a secular one. Despite the Court's efforts to clarify that its decision does not in any way allow an appeal to religion to gain votes, the fact remains that the Hindu Right will be able to continue to pursue its discursive strategy of attacking minorities through its manipulations of the discourse of secularism. It means that the Hindu Right can continue its efforts to promote enmity and hatred against Muslims in the guise of secularism. Although the Court was clear that blatantly hateful comments like those of Thackeray would not be tolerated, and would constitute a violation of the Representation of the People Act, 1951, attacks on the very legitimacy of minority rights that are dressed up in the discourse of secularism will attract no such liability.[39]

Finally, in its rejection of the review petition, the Supreme Court concluded that there was nothing inconsistent between the *Bommai* decision and the Hindutva decision.[40] There is a kernel of truth in the Court's conclusions. There is no clearly articulated principle of secularism that is undermined, no protection overruled, no earlier decision reversed. But that is not the end of the story. First, the conclusion of the Court that nothing in the *Bommai* case was of assistance in interpreting sections 3 and 3(A) of the Representation of the People Act, 1951 is unsustainable: several of the opinions in the *Bommai* decision made specific mention of these sections of the Representation

---

[39] This seems to be precisely the strategy adopted by the BJP in both its 1996 and 1998 election campaigns. It has placed the face of moderation at the front of the party, displacing and even distancing itself from the more militant faces. But at the same time, the BJP continues to campaign on its platform of secularism, which continues to include all its usual characteristics: 'One Nation, One People, One Culture', the repeal of Articles 30 and 370 of the Constitution, the introduction of a Uniform Civil Code, and the replacement of the National Minorities Commission with the National Human Rights Commission, and 'the construction of a magnificent Shri Ram Mandir at Ram Janmasthan in Ayodhya' (1998 Manifesto, p. 4).

[40] *Mohd Aslam v. Union of India*, (See Introduction, n. 3).

of the People Act, 1951 and can be seen to have set out the framework of secularism within which these sections ought to be interpreted. Moreover, a careful reading of the Hindutva decisions reveals many inconsistencies with the spirit of secularism affirmed by the Supreme Court in the earlier decision. The conclusions on the meaning of Hindutva, and on the secular nature of the speeches of the Hindu Right, are fundamentally at odds with the conclusions of the full Constitutional Bench of the Supreme Court on both the meaning and importance of secularism, and the unsecular nature of the strategies of the Hindu Right.

In *Bommai*, the declaration of presidential rule in four states following the destruction of the Babri Masjid on December 6, 1992 was challenged. The full constitutional bench of the Supreme Court upheld the validity of the declaration of presidential rule and, in so doing, passed considerable opinion on the importance and meaning of secularism in India. The opinions of four Justices, speaking on behalf of seven members of the Supreme Court, unanimously affirmed the importance of secularism to the Indian Constitution, as well as the distinctively Indian concept of secularism as equal respect for all religions.[41] Reflecting the general character of Indian secularism, each of the four opinions emphasized equal respect for all religions. For example, Justice Sawant echoed the common view that in India, secularism does not involve a complete separation of religion and the state, but rather, involves treating all religions

[41] The opinions in *Bommai*, chapter 1, n. 13, dealing with secularism were delivered by Justice Sawant (on behalf of Justice Kuldip Singh with Justice Pandian, concurring in part); Justice Jeevan Reddy, (on behalf of Justice S. C. Agarwal, with Justice Pandian also concurring in part); Justice Ramaswamy, and a brief opinion by Justice Ahmadi. Only Justices Verma and Dayal expressed no opinion on the question of secularism.

equally.[42] In his words: 'The ideal of a secular State in the sense of a State which treats all religions alike and displays benevolence towards them is in a way more suited to the Indian environment and climate than that of a truly secular State by which [is] meant a state which creates complete separation between religion and the State.'[43] According to Justice Sawant, this concept of secularism as religious tolerance and equal treatment of all religious groups included an assurance of the protection of life, property and places of worship of all religious groups. In his view, any act of a state government 'calculated to subvert or sabotage secularism as enshrined in our Constitution, can lawfully be deemed to give rise to a situation in which the Government of the State cannot be carried on in accordance with the provisions of the Constitution.'[44]

[42] Quoting and reviewing at length with approval from a 1965 lecture by M. C. Setalvad, Justice Sawant noted that secularism in India does not imply a complete separation of religion and state as in the United States. 'In our country, all religions are placed on the basis of equality.'

[43] Justice Sawant further wrote: '...Secularism under our Constitution is that whatever the attitude of the State towards the religions, religious sects and denominations, religion cannot be mixed with any secular activity of the State. In fact, the encroachment of religion into secular activities is strictly prohibited. This is evident from the provisions of the Constitution to which we have made reference above. The State's tolerance of religion or religious belief does not make it either a religious or a theocratic State. When the State allows citizens to practise and profess their religions, it does not either explicitly or implicitly allow them to introduce religion into non-religious and secular activities of the State. The freedom and tolerance of religion is only to the extent of permitting pursuit of spiritual life which is different from the secular life... This is also clear from sub-section (3) of Section 123 of the Representation of the People Act, 1951...[and] sub-section 3(A) of the same section...religious tolerance and equal treatment of all religious groups and protection of their life and property and of the places of their worship are an essential part of secularism enshrined in our Constitution' (p. 146).

[44] Ibid., para 91. Although each of the decisions echoed the general idea of Indian secularism as equal respect for all religions, there were however

In a similar vein, the opinions of Justice Jeevan Reddy and Justice Ramaswamy both condemned the strategies of the Hindu Right as non-secular. For example, Justice Jeevan Reddy stated:

...it is clear that if any party or organization seeks to fight the elections on the basis of a plank which has the proximate effect of eroding the secular philosophy of the Constitution it would certainly be guilty of following an unconstitutional course of action...Introducing religion into politics is to introduce an impermissible element into body politic and an imbalance in our constitutional system. If a political party espousing a particular religion comes to power, that religion tends to become, in practice, the official religion...This would be plainly antithetical to Arts. 14 to 16, 25 and the entire constitutional scheme adumbrated hereinabove. Under our Constitution, no party or organization can simultaneously be a political and a religious party.[45]

Justice Ramaswamy's decision also strongly condemned the rise of fundamentalism as a violation of the constitutional principle of secularism. For example, he wrote: 'Rise of fundamentalism and communalization of politics are anti-secularism. They encourage separatist and divisive forces and become breeding

---

slightly different emphases in each of the decisions. For example, while Justice Sawant most strongly emphasized equal respect for all religions, and its requirement of toleration, Jeevan Reddy's decision placed some emphasis on the idea of the separation of religion and politics. After a long discussion of the requirement of equal respect, Justice Jeevan Reddy stated: 'In short, in the affairs of the State religion is irrelevant; it is strictly a personal affair. In this sense...our Constitution is broadly in agreement with the U.S. Constitution, the First Amendment whereof declares that "Congress shall make no laws respecting an establishment of religion or prohibiting the free exercise thereof...". Perhaps, this is an echo of the doctrine of separation of Church and State; maybe it is the modern political thought which seeks to separate religion from the State—it matters very little.' By way of contrast again, Justice Ramaswamy's opinion, while also speaking of equal respect for all religions, included several references to the concept of neutrality.

[45] Ibid.

grounds for national disintegration and fail the Parliamentary democratic system and the Constitution.'[46]

In stark contrast to the views expressed by the Court in the Hindutva case, the Court in *Bommai* recognized that the BJP's strategy was one of attacking the right to freedom of religion of the minorities, and thus, of undermining one of the very essentials of secularism. Perhaps because of the extremity of the situation at hand—the destruction of the mosque, the outbreak of communal riots and the declaration of presidential rule—the Court in *Bommai* was not blinded by the discourse of secularism used by the Hindu Right to advance its agenda. But in the Hindutva cases, it was the *discourse* that was effectively on trial. It was the discursive strategies—of promoting Hindutva, of attacking minorities through the language of secularism and equality, as well as through more extremist hate speech, that was at issue. Had the Supreme Court been willing to critically examine this discourse—to examine the meaning of Hindutva and its implications for minorities, as well as the way in which the political aspirations of Hindutva are now cloaked in the rhetoric of secularism—it would have been able to see the extent to which the Hindu Right was undermining the very essentials of secularism. The critical flaw, in both the Hindutva decisions and in the subsequent dismissal of the review petition, was the failure to critically examine this discourse. Contrary to the conclusion of the Court in the review petition, a more critical and detailed analysis should have revealed that the 'apprehensions and misgivings expressed in the writ petition' were anything but 'imaginary and baseless'.[47]

At the same time, it is important to recognize that the conclusions of the Supreme Court in the *Manohar Joshi* case

[46] Ibid., para 132.
[47] See chapter 2, pp 24–5.

were at least partially facilitated by the fact that the Constitutional Bench in the *Bommai* decision did not articulate the precise meaning of the concept of equal respect for all religions. The pronouncements of the Supreme Court in *Bommai* were important affirmations of the principle of secularism, and equally important denunciations of the communalism of the Hindu Right. However, the decision remains marred by the elusive nature of the underlying conception of equality, and the kind of state action mandated by this conception. It is partially because the meaning of equality remains unarticulated that the Hindu Right can continue to advance its position as a legitimate version of secularism, and that the Supreme Court can condone its position as such. Similarly, as we will discuss in the next section, the unarticulated nature of the underlying conceptions of freedom of religion and toleration also contribute to the spurious manner in which the Hindu Right has cloaked itself in a veil of secularism. We do not mean to suggest that the courts alone are responsible for this increasing legitimacy of the claims of the Hindu Right to secularism, nor that the courts alone will be able to reverse the trend. However, we do believe that the courts can help uphold the principle of secularism by more carefully and precisely articulating the content of equal respect for all religions, and in so doing, may at least be able to close the doors on any further constitutional recognition of the Hindu Right's claim to secularism.

5

Secularism in Crisis

The sheer instability of the secular as a cultural and legal category needs
to be acknowledged as the new point of departure for elaborating on
secularism(s) in India today.

*Rustom Bharucha**

The rise of the Hindu Right in and through the discourse
of secularism has intensified the contemporary debates
on the concept of secularism in India. Despite the
widespread agreement within constitutional discourse of secularism as a cornerstone of Indian democracy as well as its
distinctive Indian character as equal respect for all religions,
secularism remains a highly contested concept. Some critics
reject the concept of secularism altogether, arguing that it is
wholly derived from western modernity, and ill-suited to the
historical realities of Indian society. Others come to secularism's
defense, but are highly critical of the evolution of secularism

* Rustom Bharucha, *In the Name of Secular: Cultural Interactions and
Interventions,* EPW (Nov 5, 1994), p. 2925

in and through the Indian State. Yet others, in a related vein, argue for a reconceptualization of secularism within the Indian polity. In this chapter, we briefly review these different trajectories of the debate over the (non)-rightful place of secularism in India, and attempt to situate our own project of recuperating a notion of democratic secularism within it. We then sketch out the principles that we believe might provide a framework for rethinking and recuperating a vision of democratic secularism.

A number of critics—the *agents provocateurs* of secularism[1]—have argued that the project of secularism ought to be abandoned altogether. Ashis Nandy, who has led this intellectual charge, defiantly proclaims 'I am not a secularist. In fact, I can be called an anti-secularist'.[2] He sets out to recover 'a well-known domain of public concern in South Asia, ethnic and especially religious tolerance, from the hegemonic language of secularism popularized by westernized intellectuals and middle classes exposed to the globally dominant languages of the nation-state in this part of the world.'[3] He argues that religion has been bifurcated into faith (a way of life) and ideology (a political or socio-economic claim based on religion). Secularism, an import from nineteenth century Europe, views religion as ideology, and casts it as opposed to the modernizing ideology of the modern state. This secularism, which calls for an area of public life where religion has no place, that is, for a separation of religion and politics, has in Nandy's view, exhausted its possibilities in India. At the same time, Nandy acknowledges a second, non-western meaning of

[1] Bhargava, Ibid.

[2] See Ashis Nandy, 'The Politics of Secularism and the Recovery of Religious Tolerance', *Alternatives* XIII (April 1988), reprinted in Bhargava, ed., chapter 3, n. 5. See also, 'An Anti-Secularist Manifesto', *Seminar* (October 1985).

[3] Nandy, ibid., p. 58.

secularism: the equal respect for all religions. This accommoda-tive and pluralist vision of secularism is, according to Nandy, more compatible with the meaning that the majority of Indians give to secularism. But it is the other meaning of secularism that is advocated by the country's westernized intellectuals and, more dangerously, which is 'supported by the accelerating process of modernization in India.' Nandy argues that this ideology of secularism, alongside the ideologies of nationalism and develop-ment, has become intolerant, coercive, even violent.[4]

Rather than relying on the secularism of the modernized elite, Nandy argues that Indians should 'explore the philosophy, the symbolism and the theology of tolerance in the various faiths of the citizens and hope that the state systems in South Asia may learn something about religious tolerance from everyday Hinduism, Islam, Buddhism, and/or Sikhism...'[5] It is this pre-modern religious tolerance, as seen in Gandhi's anti-secular and anti-modernist legacy, that Nandy wants to recuperate. It is a tolerance not only of religion, but a 'tolerance that is religious', and therefore, a tolerance that is located 'outside the ideological grid of modernity'.[6]

Some of this critique is echoed in the work of T. N. Madan, who has argued that secularism in India is impossible as a shared vision, impracticable as a basis for state action, and impotent as a blueprint for the future.[7] According to Madan, it is the very

[4] Nandy argues that 'while the modern state builds up pressures on citizens to give up their faith in public, it guarantees no protection to them against the sufferings inflicted by the state itself in the name of its ideology. On the contrary, with the help of modern communications and the secular coercive power at its command, the state frequently uses its ideology to silence its non-conforming citizens.' Ibid.

[5] Ibid. [6] Ibid.

[7] T. N. Madan, 'Secularism in its Place', *Journal of Asian Studies*, 46:4, (November 1987) pp 747–8, reprinted in Bhargava (ed.), chapter 3, n. 5. Madan

disavowal of religion within secularism that has facilitated the rise of Hindu nationalism and other religious extremism, by denying 'the very legitimacy of religion in human life and society'.[8] Despite the continuing progress of secularization (which, following Peter Berger, is defined as 'the process by which sectors of society and culture are removed from the domination of religious institutions and symbols', Madan argues that secularism has failed to make headway in India. In his view, secularism is 'a gift of Christianity' and a product of the Enlightenment, built into the western model of development and modernization—a model that has not been readily translatable or transferable to the cultural histories and traditions of South Asia.

But at the same time, Madan's message is not one of outright rejection. 'Secularism must be put in its place: which is not a question of rejecting it but of finding the proper means for its expression.'[9] Like Nandy, Madan also turns to the Gandhian understanding of the appropriate relationship between religion and politics, which emphasizes inter-religious understanding as well as 'a spiritually justified limitation of the role of religious institutions and symbols in certain areas of contemporary

---

argues that secularism 'is impossible as a credo for life because the great majority of the people of South Asia are, in their own eyes, active adherents of some religious faith. It is impracticable as a basis for state action either because Buddhism or Islam have been declared state or state-protected religions, or because the stance of religious neutrality or equidistance is difficult to maintain since religious minorities do not share the majority's view of what this entails for the state. And it is impotent as a blueprint for the future because, by its very nature, it is incapable of countering religious fundamentalism and fanaticism'. See also, 'Whither Indian Secularism?' *Modern Asian Studies*, 27:3 (1993), p. 667.

[8] Madan, *Secularism in its Place*, op. cit., p. 757.

[9] Peter Berger, *The Social Reality of Religion* (London: Allen Lane, 1973), as quoted in Madan.

life'.[10] Madan concludes with the observation that the only way that secularism will succeed in South Asia is if both religion and secularism are taken seriously. In a later essay, he similarly concludes his critique not with outright rejection, but with a call for rethinking.[11]

A decentralized polity, a positive attitude towards cultural pluralism, and a genuine concern and respect for human rights would be, perhaps, the best guarantors of Indian secularism, understood as inter–religious understanding in a society and the state policy of non-discrimination and of equal distance (*not* equal proximity) from the religious concerns of the people.[12]

His critique is, then, ultimately a weaker version than Nandy's. Although concerned with the adaptability of western models of secularism to the South Asian cultural context, he stops short of a complete rejection of secularism. Rather, although offering no conclusions or blueprints, Madan seems to lean in the direction of retrieving secularism through a Gandhian understanding of inter-religious tolerance.

In a critique not entirely unsympathetic to the Madan/ Nandy thesis, Partha Chatterjee has argued for a reconfiguration of the problem of secularism to one of toleration.[13] In his view,

[10] Ibid., p. 757.

[11] Madan, 'Whither Indian Secularism?', above, n. 7.

[12] Ibid. In a 'Postscript' to 'Secularism in its Place', written ten years after the original article, Madan again emphasized that it was not his intention to reject secularism outright, but rather, to subject prevailing and overly complacent conceptions of secularism to critique. 'To draw attention to the limitations of the original ideology of secularism and its Indian versions does not necessarily imply that one rejects them. Critiques may well result in strengthening the institutions concerned if the necessary corrective or reinforcing measures are carefully put in place.' Madan, Postscript in Bhargava (ed.), chapter 3, n. 5, p. 318.

[13] Partha Chatterjee, 'Secularism and Toleration', *EPW* (July 9, 1994), p. 1768.

the challenge presented by the Hindu Right must be understood
not primarily as one of secularism but rather, as one of minority
rights. Accordingly, he argues that what is needed to meet this
challenge is a reconceptualization of the concept of toleration.
He raises similar doubts as Nandy as to 'whether secularism
necessarily ensures toleration'. But in contrast to Nandy who
seeks toleration in the cultural traditions of pre-modern India,
Chatterjee sets out to find a political conception of toleration.
Chatterjee's concern is not so much with the western or modern
roots of secularism, but rather with its liberal democratic roots.
In his view, liberal democratic theory, and therefore secularism,
is ultimately unable to meet the challenge of group rights.
Chatterjee then argues for a reconceptualization of the concept
of toleration, as the basis for the recognition and accommodation of group rights in general, and minority religious rights in
particular.[14]

The critique of secularism has not gone unanswered, and
many commentators continue to defend a secular vision of
India. It is argued that secularism has exhausted neither its
normative nor political possibilities in India. Some argue in
favour of more separation between State and religion, others for
a reconceptualized version of secularism, more in keeping with
the distinctive nature of the Indian polity. Yet others simply
defend secularism from its detractors. Despite their many
internal differences, these commentators all take issue with the
Madan/Nandy critique, and share the view that secularism has

[14] Nandy, Madan and Chatterjee all share a commitment to the principle
of toleration, and a diagnosis of the contemporary ills of India as an erosion
of the toleration of differences, and all share the view that secularism has
exhausted its capacity for delivering on this principle. But they differ in where
they search for an alternative. While Nandy and Madan look to India's
religious past, Chatterjee looks to India's political future.

not yet exhausted its conceptual or political possibilities. All are uncompromising in their defence of the place of secularism in India, despite their differences on the way in which this secularism should unfold. Amartya Sen, for example, in an unequivocal defence of the rightful place of secularism in India has argued that:

...[secularism] is in fact, a part of a more comprehensive idea—that of India as an integrally pluralist country, made up of different religious beliefs, distinct language groups, divergent social practices. Secularism is one aspect—a very important one—of the recognition of that larger idea of heterogeneous identity... Given the diversity and contrast within India, there is not, in the comprehensive politics of the country, much alternative to secularism as an essential part of overall pluralism.[15]

Many of the commentators, who have come to secularism's defence, nevertheless remain highly critical of the way in which secularism has evolved in the Indian context. Rajeev Bhargava, for example, argues for a contextual secularism, which does not require strict non-interference, mutual exclusion or equidistance, but rather a policy of principled distance.[16] According to

[15] Amartya Sen, 'The Threats to Secular India' 60:7 *The New York Times Review of Books* XL-7 26 (April 8, 1993). See also Sen 'Secularism and its Discontents' in Bhargava (ed.), chapter 3, n. 5, where Sen offers arguments against six distinct strands of critique against secularism. Sen does not suggest that secularism is trouble-free, but rather, that any re-examination of the difficult questions that arise from the principle of symmetrical treatment of different religious communities must occur within a commitment to secularism. He concludes that '...the case for re-examining...does not contradict the overarching argument for secularism and the overwhelming need for symmetric treatment of different communities and religions in India... The winter of our discontent might not be giving way, right now, to a "glorious summer", but the abandonment of secularism would make things far more wintry than they currently are' (ibid., p. 485).

[16] See Bhargava, 'Giving Secularism its Due', *EPW* (July 9, 1994) and 'What is Secularism For?' in Bhargava (ed.), *Secularism and its Critics* 1998.

Bhargava, the 'dominant justification of the policies and practices of the Indian state was done by appealing to contextual secularism of the principled distance variety; exclude religion for some purposes and include it to achieve other objectives, but always out of non-sectarian considerations.'[17] But he argues that there has been a degeneration of this contextual secularism by the Indian state, with sectarian considerations increasingly relevant. 'It has let religion enter politics when it ought to have excluded it, excluded religion when much could have been achieved by inclusion each time on sectarian grounds. The crisis of Indian secularism is undoubtedly real, but not because of conceptual flaws inherent in its theoretical structure'.[18]

Yet others question the appropriateness of the particular model of secularism, arguing that Indian democracy might be better served by a more complete separation of religion and politics.[19] Upadhyaya, for example, has argued that the concept of *sarva dharma samabhava* has failed to transcend the categories of communalism and that this approach to secularism has been an underlying cause of the communalization of Indian politics. In his view, this understanding of secularism which envisions the state as 'the representative body of all religious communities' becomes a majoritarian secularism. Upadhyaya argues that if all communities within this approach to secularism were to be equal

[17] Bhargava, ibid., p. 521.

[18] Akeel Bilgrami is similarly critical of the way in which secularism has developed in India. In 'Two Concepts of Secularism: Reason, Modernity and Archimedean Ideal', *EPW* (July 4, 1994), p. 1749, he argues that the Archimedean secularism of Nehru should be displaced by a negotiated secularism, that is, one that could emerge 'by negotiation between the substantive commitments of particular religious communities.'

[19] See Prakash Chandra Upadhyaya 'The Politics of Indian Secularism' 26:4 *Modern Asian Studies* (1992) 815, who argues that equal respect for all religions has been responsible for communalising politics.

'one would be more equal than others—namely, the majority "Hindu community".' This approach, he argues, has given rise to a majoritarian politics in which 'representative politics based on adult franchise have become a contest in which communities are mobilized in a competition for votes, and in which the majority community must always win.' The major lacunae in the conceptualization of secularism in India thus 'lies in the definition of secularism...in that secularism has not been clearly defined in terms of the separation of religion from politics, either in its constitutional form or in the conventions of the political process.'[20] Thus, in striking contrast to not only the critics of secularism, but also those who defend its distinctive Indian character as equal respect for all religions, Upadhyaya unapologetically calls for more separation between religion and politics.

The secularism debate in India has been rigorous, passionate, and often, highly polarized. But notwithstanding the antagonisms, there are some shared concerns. Many of the detractors of secularism as well as its champions share an underlying

---

[20] Ibid. In his view, Indian secularism has been co-opted 'by communal parties and ideologies in this way because it has never meant the separation of religion from politics. Instead, it defines religion and community as legitimate platforms for political mobilization, and merely preaches political accommodation between all religious communities. This is a definition that is open to interpretation and misrepresentation, and allows communalists to masquerade as secularists' (p. 852). Upadhyaya, however, also emphasizes the important differences between majoritarianism and communalism. Majoritarianism 'represents accommodation and moderation as opposed to confrontation with minorities. It preaches not religious orthodoxy but religious heterodoxy. It maintains a semblance of tolerance as opposed to the outright intolerance of the communalist. It seeks to replace the language of religious antagonism with the vocabulary of non-antagonistic communalism.' But despite these important differences, he concludes that 'at moments of communal polarization, majoritarian secularism is always in danger of being swamped by Hindu communalism' (Ibid.).

concern with the principle of tolerance, and its erosion in the context of contemporary India. But the critics diverge in their views on where to search for this principle. Nandy and Madan look to pre-modern India, and to the religions of South Asia, while Chatterjee looks to develop a political conception of toleration, derived from his Foucauldian analysis of governance. By contrast, Upadhyaya speaks of countering majoritarianism in a more complete separation of religion and politics within secularism—a quest which similarly amounts to a plea for a more substantive toleration of religious minorities. And others look to recuperate the Indian conception of equal respect for all religions. In a closely related vein, there is a shared apprehension of the escalation of communal tensions, particularly in light of the recent rise of the Hindu Right. Despite the inflammatory rhetoric that has at times characterized the debate, none of these critics are accurately described as communal. Nandy and Sen, Chatterjee and Bilgrami, all seem equally troubled by the intolerance, antagonisms, and hatred promoted in and through communalism. Again, these critics differ in their diagnosis of these symptoms, with Nandy laying the blame with modernity, and others like Bilgrami suggesting that the authoritarianism of the Nehruvian state is at fault. But all are agreed in their normative evaluation of communalism. Finally, many of the critics also share an underlying concern with the erosion of the normative and political commitment to the basic democratic principle of protecting minority rights. Although the language of rights and democracy is undoubtedly too modern for Nandy's taste, Chatterjee and Bilgrami for example, seem equally disturbed with the erosion of this democratic principle.[21]

[21] It is also important to recognize that as the debate has evolved, it has become increasingly sophisticated, with a number of the critics of both sides acknowledging the important critical insights provided by their opponents.

There is, then, a minimal consensus that the current crisis of secularism is related to the erosion of toleration, the upsurge of Hindu majoritarianism, and the increasing disregard of the rights of minorities. Where the consensus quickly breaks down is whether the concept of secularism is up to the challenge of reversing the tides, or partially responsible for the rather dismal current state of affairs. The debate remains sharply divided on this central question. Is secularism normatively desirable and politically viable in India today? Is it capable of providing a conceptual and/or political basis for the promotion of toleration and a basic respect of difference?

It is on this fault line that we firmly locate ourselves on the side of secularism. We believe that the principle of secularism remains an important normative commitment, and that its political viability, although not a foregone conclusion, is well worth fighting for. We agree that turning the tide of intolerance is a tall order for the concept of secularism. Admittedly, secularism alone is probably incapable of rooting out what has become a deeply institutionalized pathology. The erosion of tolerance is rooted in a multiplicity of other dominant ideologies and institutions including, according to almost all critics, the State itself. Neither are we so idealistic as to believe that normative political concepts are possessed of magic powers whereby they can simply transform these dominant ideologies. But we do believe that such concepts have become sites of discursive struggle, on which these ideologies are contested. To

---

Madan, for example, has responded to many of the criticisms of his initial article, and in his recent 'Postscript' has attempted to achieve more precision and nuance in his critique of secularism. Similarly Bhargava, a staunch defender of secularism, notes that there is much critical bite in the Nandy/Madan thesis, and that those committed to revitalizing secularism must take note of its many weaknesses.

abandon the discourse of secularism would be to concede this site of discursive struggle not simply to the *agents provocateurs* of secularism but, much more significantly, to the forces of Hindu majoritarianism, namely, the Hindu Right. While the secularism debate has produced important critical insights into the limitations of current modes of secular politics which must be taken into account, there is little to be gained by abdicating the terrain entirely. The idea that pre-modern forms will provide some alternative to the contemporary crisis is, as many of Nandy's critics have persuasively argued, little more than nostalgic idealism.[22] Although the critique of modernity is powerful and at times insightful, it does not lend itself to political prescriptions of 'return'.[23]

Although the critique may rightly call for a critical engagement with modernity and a deconstructive relationship with many of its normative commitments like secularism, its modality is inescapable. Indeed, even Chatterjee, who critically engages with secularism, nevertheless recognizes that the struggle for toleration and the protection of minority rights is a political struggle that will be fought out on the terrain of modernity. As postcolonial theory has so amply demonstrated, the encounter with modernity and colonialism has irrevocably transformed

---

[22] See, for example, Bhargava (ed.), chapter 3, n. 5, and Thomas Pantham, 'Indian Secularism and its Critics: Some Reflections', *The Review of Politics*, 59:3, (1997), p. 523.

[23] As Pantham, ibid., argues 'A wholesale rejection of modernity and a nostalgic yearning for the so-called nonpolitical religious tolerance of the past may inhibit us from finding or constructing emancipatory or transformative practices from within our effective, modern history' (p. 538). Citing Sudipta Kaviraj who argues that 'the logic of modernity pervades the map of identities', Pantham further argues that modernity leaves 'no identity untouched. What this view implies is that under modernity any notion of emancipatory or transformative agency has necessarily to be political'.

Indian cultural and political categories. There is no return to a space of pure Indian culture, uncontaminated by the colonial and postcolonial encounter. This is not to suggest that there is no value in seeking to promote political norms/praxis that resonate with Indian cultural traditions. On the contrary, the postcolonial critique suggests that in many ways, the political values and practices of western modernity have already been hybridized in just such a way: secularism is a case in point. The dominant meaning of secularism in India is unrecognizable to many a western eye.[24] The idea of equal respect for all religions as governing the relationship between religion and politics is not an idea that is obviously derived from the Enlightenment notion of secularization, and the separation of religion and politics.[25]

We simply do not believe that the norm of secularism—in its Indian hybridized form—has exhausted its political possibilities. But in taking this position, we join those critics who are attempting to bridge the gap within the debate, by taking on board at least some of the critical insights of those on the other side. We join those whose work is committed to the search for a middle ground of secularism, working within the Indian conception of secularism, while rethinking the norm at its limits. Further, we enter into these debates with a focus on the constitutional discourses of secularism, that is, on the legal and specifically constitutional discourses articulated by the courts. Those who believe that the State is inherently part of the problem may dismiss our focus on law, as an official state

[24] See Smith (1964) chapter 4, n. 7, and others, who argue that Indian is not a secular state, according to western liberal democratic conceptions of the secular.

[25] Though as a number of commentators have observed, the western notion of secularism is less monolithic than the critics of secularism would have us believe. Bhargava, for example, attempts to illustrate the extent to which the idea of equal respect can be derived from a western tradition of secularism.

discourse, as politically naïve.[26] But our engagement with law is not intended to suggest that legal discourse alone can turn the current majoritarian tides, which continue to erode the very foundations of toleration. We do not come to law with delusions of its grandeur. As we have argued elsewhere, we see the law neither as an instrument of liberation nor one of oppression, but rather, as a complex and contradictory site, on which competing visions of the world are fought out.[27] We recognize the law's often paradoxical role, as an official state discourse deeply implicated in its dominant ideologies and practices, yet by virtue of its need for legitimacy, autonomous enough to sometimes challenge such state practices. A critical analysis of law requires a critique of the State; but a critique of the State need not lead to an abandonment of law. An abandonment of law is as dangerous, in our view, as an abandonment of secularism. Despite its limitations as a site of political transformation, it remains an important site of struggle, and to abandon law would be to concede it to conservative political forces, including those of the Hindu Right.

Our focus on this constitutional discourse is, then, simply in recognition of the extent to which law itself has become an important site of discursive struggle over the meaning of secularism, and the broader contest over the role and status of minorities in India. To the extent that law itself has become a

[26] Many in the secularism debate share a critique of the nation state—not shared in content, but rather in focus. Many commentators see the particular evolution of the modern nation state as implicated in the crisis of secularism, and argue that a critique of the state—that is, a critique of the ways in which secularism has played out in and through the nation state—is necessary to understand this crisis. Some are more critical of the State itself, while others retain a more liberal and trusting approach, arguing simply for its de-communalization.

[27] See Kapur and Cossman, *Subversive Sites*, (1996) Introduction, n. 1.

site of this struggle, it is important for the forces of democratic secularism to engage on this, as well as other, terrain(s). As such, the courts can play a role in this broader discursive struggle over the meaning of secularism, and the place of minorities. At the least, the courts can guard against any further legal erosion of the principle of toleration and the rights of minorities. Beyond this basic minimum, the courts could also play a significant role in more precisely articulating the principles and content of democratic secularism in India.

It is with this limited, but important role of legal discourse in mind, that we turn to briefly reconsider the principles that ought to inform democratic secularism, principles designed with a view to promoting toleration, and constraining the majoritarianism of the Indian political scene. We situate this project within the dominant discourse of secularism, that is, of equal respect for all religions. Our focus on this discourse follows in part from our focus on the dominant legal and constitutional approaches which have long defined Indian secularism as equal respect for all religions. But our focus on this version of secularism is also principled. We do not believe that the various critiques of this model have been persuasive.

First, this model of secularism—equal respect for all religions—has not been persuasively negated by the anti-secularist critique. Nandy, for example, recognizes the competing models of secularism in India—the separation thesis advocated by westernized intellectuals and the accommodative thesis accepted by the majority of Indians.[28] But having recognized these two models, Nandy appears to focus his critical attention only on the first. By obscuring the very distinction that he initially recognizes, Nandy avoids addressing the question of why the

---

[28] Nandy, 'The Politics of Secularism', (1998) above, n. 2.

accommodative thesis is not up to the challenge of promoting secularism. Nandy's message about toleration is well worth noting. Like Chatterjee, Nandy's objective of promoting tolera- tion is a laudable one. But there is simply no answer— satisfactory or otherwise—to the question of why the Indian version of secularism—the equal respect for all religions—is not up to this task. Rather Nandy appears content to focus his ire on modernity, and with a sleight of hand, secularism, violence and modernity are elided into a singular totalizing enemy.[29] We do not agree with Nandy that attention to the complex role of religion in India and to the need to promote toleration neces- sarily requires such a complete rejection of the secular alterna- tive.

Similarly, we do not agree with Chatterjee that attention to the problems of majoritarianism and toleration necessarily require a shift *away* from secularism. Chatterjee seems to accept the liberal democratic version of secularism and its requirements of neutrality as the definition against which Indian secularism is to be judged, and ultimately found lacking since it cannot meet the requirements of neutrality. In shifting the focus to the principle of toleration, Chatterjee, like Nandy, glosses over the fact that this principle of toleration has become the third defining feature of Indian secularism, particularly within the

---

[29] Bhargava has similarly argued that 'The difficulty is that although he [Nandy] works with two forms of secularism, he possesses only one version of modernity. And since he rejects that modernity, he is left in the end not with an alternative version of modern secularism but with notions of tolerance that rely exclusively on traditional religion'. Bhargava argues that there is in fact 'space within [Nandy's] writings for an alternative proposal consistent with modern secularism', that is, that within the Indian accommodative model, there is room for the kind of 'continuous dialogue among religious traditions' that Nandy otherwise advocates, despite Nandy's own slamming of the secular door (Bhargava, 1998, chapter 3, n. 5, p. 525).

context of constitutional discourse. The choice need not be cast as one between secularism and toleration, since the specific variety of Indian secularism has long been said to be informed by the principle of toleration. By the same token, we *do* agree that any principled defence of Indian secularism must include a refocusing on toleration. Toleration needs to be wrestled away from its current majoritarianism moorings, and revitalized with a sense of democratic protection for cultural minorities, and cultural pluralism. In our view, some of Chatterjee's suggestions for a rethinking of the principle of toleration may nevertheless be useful *within* the context of a democratic revitalization of the concept of secularism itself. We will elaborate on this rethinking of the concept of toleration further below.

Secondly, we do not believe that this model of secularism has been persuasively negated by critics like Upadhayaya who argue for a more complete separation of religion and politics. Although a strong normative claim for a more complete delinking of religion and politics could certainly be made, it hardly seems any more likely in the current political environment than it was in Nehru's day. In our view, any effort to argue for a wall of separation of religion and politics at the current juncture will invariably fall into the trap of 'westernization', that is, it will simply be written off as a misguided effort to impose a western model of secularism onto the highly distinctive character of Indian society. It is not only the opponents of secularism like Nandy who would dismiss such claims, but also all those who defend the dominant discourse of secularism in India as equal respect for all religions.

Beyond this pragmatic limitation, there is reason to question the conceptual possibilities of a model of secularism that advocates a more complete separation of religion and politics. There is no reason to believe that a radical conceptual shift to a separation of religion and politics will be able to meet the challenge of majoritarianism. In the American context, where the establishment clause in the First Amendment to the U.S. Constitution requires state non-intervention in religion,[30] it is not at all clear that this majoritarianism has been avoided.[31] Rather, many critics have argued that the requirement of state non-intervention and neutrality on issues of religion has in fact served to reinforce the power relations of the status quo, and thus the dominant position of religious majorities. For example, in one decision of the U.S. Supreme Court, the Sunday closing laws were challenged by religious minorities whose Sabbath (weekly day of rest) fell on a day other than Sunday, as violating their right to freedom of religion and the anti-establishment clause.[32] They argued that they should be allowed to close on their Sabbath, and remain open on Sundays. The Court upheld the constitutionality of the Sunday closings. While conceding that such laws were originally religious in nature, the Court held that the present purpose and effect of these laws was to impose a uniform, and neutral day of rest for all citizens. The fact that this uniform day of rest was of particular significance to Christians was not considered to be an obstacle to this secular

---

[30] Although the idea of a wall of separation goes back to the words of Jefferson, it was only given judicial expression as a basic principle of constitutional law by the United States Supreme Court in the 1940s. In *Everson v. Board of Education of Ewing Township* 330 US 1 (1947), Justice Black, writing for the majority, emphasized the requirement of strict government neutrality on issues of religion.

[31] Indeed, very few commentators appear to be of the view that there really is a wall of separation between religion and the State in the United States. Despite the anti-establishment clause, there are in fact a broad range of widely accepted state-sanctioned religious activities, which include the United States currency which proudly displays 'In God We Trust', opening prayers at state assemblies, and state funding of chaplains in the armed forces.

[32] *McGowan v. Maryland* 266 US 420 1961

objective.[33] The case reveals how in the name of secularism, the dominant norms of the Christian majority were reinforced at the expense of the norms of the minority.[34]

A similar majoritarian religious bias is evident in the case of *Lynch v. Donnelly* which held that the public display of a creche (the nativity scene of Jesus, displayed during Christmas) does not violate the establishment clause.[35] The Supreme Court held that 'The City... has principally taken note of a significant historical religious event long celebrated in the Western World... The display is sponsored by the City to celebrate the Holiday and to depict the origins of that Holiday. These are legitimate secular purposes.' In this reasoning, the explicitly Christian religious holiday has apparently become so invisible from the unstated norm of the majority that the Court can simply claim the holiday to be secular in nature. Again, in the name of neutrality, the dominant norms of the Christian majority were reinforced.

[33] In a later decision of *Thornton v. Caldor, Inc.* 474 US 703 (1985), the Supreme Court struck down a Connecticut law that allowed Sabbath observers the right to not work on their Sabbath. In the Court's view, the fact that only Sabbath observers had the right to designate their day off (other workers simply had the right to a day off, but not to designate that day) was a violation of the constitutional requirement of neutrality. As a result, the State can force all individuals to take off Sunday (the traditional Christian Sabbath) as long as it does not do so in the name of the Sabbath, but cannot accommodate the Sabbath of non-Christian observers.

[34] The dissenting opinion of Mr Justice William Douglas recognized this implicit majoritarianism: 'No matter what is said, the parentage of [the Sunday closing] laws is the Fourth Commandment... They serve and satisfy the religious predispositions of our Christian communities' (ibid., pp 572–3).

[35] *Lynch v. Donnelly* 465 US 668. The case was later distinguished by the Court in *Allegheny v. American Civil Liberties Union* 492 US 573 (1989), where Justice Sandra Day O'Connor held that a city display of a menorah alongside a Christmas tree did not endorse religion, but was simply an expression of religious plurality.

Based on such decisions, Martha Minow has argued that 'Neutral means might not produce neutral results, given historic practices and social arrangements that have not been neutral.'[36] Neutrality risks reinforcing non-neutral norms. Practices that may appear to be neutral as between different religions may in fact be premised on the norms and practices of the majority. In the face of divergent practices between majority and minority groups, state neutrality has served to reinforce the majority practices, and the power of the majority to define the norm. The majority's practices become the unquestioned norm, against which any difference is measured, and in turn defined. As Stephen Feldman has similarly argued, '[t]he legal discourse of the religion clauses contributes to this cultural imperialism by construing or labelling oppressive Christian displays and revelries as secular or as protected private sphere activities'[37] (at 859). The principle of neutrality is thus revealed to support a project of majoritarianism. In Feldman's words: 'In a hegemonically

[36] Martha Minow, *Justice Engendered*, (1987).

[37] Stephen M. Feldman, 'Principle, History, and Power: The Limits of First Amendment Religion Clauses' *Iowa Law Review* 81 (1996), p. 833. Feldman reviews a number of cases that in his view reveal the Christian bias of First Amendment jurisprudence. For example, in *Capitol Square Review and Advisory Board v. Pinette*, the Klu Klux Klan put up a latin cross on a public square. The Court held that the action was a private expression of religious belief, and thus not in violation of the First Amendment. However, in the case of *Employment Division, Oregon Department of Human Resources v. Smith*, (1990), the supervised consumption of peyote in Native American Church was not permitted. This private expression was not protected by the freedom of religion clause. Rather, according to the Court, 'the rights of free exercise do not relieve an individual of the obligation to comply with a valid and neutral law of general applicability'. According to Feldman, 'If these two cases are read together in the context of American society, they suggest that the Free Exercise Clause extends 'preferential' treatment to the 'majority's'(Christian) religious expression and beliefs' (ibid., p. 860).

Christian society ... "neutrality" equals Christianity.'[38] The turn then to a strict separation of religion and politics, and its requirement of state neutrality does not appear to have resolved the problem of majoritarianism in the American context, and there is little reason to believe that it would fare any better in the Indian context.

We are left then with a dilemma. Both the principle of toleration which underlies equal respect for all religions, and the principle of neutrality that underlies the separation of religion and politics have been shown by their critics to reinforce majoritarianism. Resolving the dilemma may lie in confronting it directly, that is, in recognizing that not only does religion remain present in the various models of secularism, but that the unstated norm of the dominant religion also remains present. The best course of action may be to adopt a model of secularism that is best able to acknowledge this dilemma. In our view, a model premised on the separation thesis is least likely to acknowledge the presence of religion, since its very premise is the prohibition of religion in politics. The model based on the accommodation thesis, by contrast, although also complicit in majoritarian politics, may be able to meet the challenge in so far as it does acknowledge the presence of religion in politics. This model can use its own premise of the *equal* treatment of all religions, as the basis for its own internal critique. That is, it can use the principle of equality to critique the way in which this model of secularism has been applied in a way that has, in fact, undermined the equality of religious minorities. We will elaborate further on the requisite rethinking of the concept of equality below.

For these various reasons, rather than calling for a more complete separation of religion and politics, we begin within the

[38] Ibid., p. 873.

dominant discourse of secularism as equal respect for all religions. Our objective is, then, to look for political, and more specifically, legal possibilities within existing constitutional discourse. We believe that it is possible to revitalize the principles that have informed this vision to better promote toleration and meet the challenge of majoritarianism. In this concluding section, we set out some tentative suggestions for working in and through the dominant discourse of secularism, in an attempt to revitalize this discourse with democratic principles. We examine each of the three basic tenets of secularism: equality, freedom of religion and toleration. Due to the centrality of the principle of toleration in the Indian conception of secularism, the bulk of our discussion is focused on this principle.

EQUALITY

First, a democratic revisioning of the principle of equal respect for all religions requires a shift in the underlying model of equality. The discourse of secularism needs to be reframed within a model of substantive equality. As we have argued elsewhere, a substantive model of equality would allow for a recognition of the claim of minorities to differential treatment.[39] A substantive model of equality directs attention to both historic and systemic forms of discrimination. In order to compensate for past and continuing disadvantage, these minorities may be treated differently. Further, a substantive model of equality can take differences into account in a way that a formal model of equality cannot. Formal equality simply insists on equal treatment; on 'treating likes alike'. In constitutional discourse, this model of equality is articulated in terms of the similarly situated test; that is, only those who are similarly

[39] See Kapur and Cossman, 1993 and 1996, Introduction, n. 1.

situated need to be treated similarly. Equality then becomes all about classification, of legally pigeon-holing those who are the same and those who are different. Within this formal model, difference then operates either to deny the very claim to equality of groups who are different (only those who are similarly situated need to be treated the same)[40], or to deny the relevance of the differences of the group (equality demands that they be treated the same). In the context of Indian secularism, the formal equality of the Hindu Right has done the latter, that is, it has insisted that religious minorities be treated the same. The question that goes unaddressed in this model of equality is 'the same as who?' A model of equality that insists on sameness invariably judges those who are different according to the unstated norms of the majority. Thus, in the context of the Hindu Right, the formal model of equality judges religious minorities according to the unstated (and in the more extreme RSS and Shiv Sena rhetoric, sometimes explicitly stated) norms of the Hindu majority. It is one of a number of ways in which the Hindu Right attempts to provide some degree of constitutional validity to its unbridled majoritarianism.

In stark contrast, a substantive approach to equality considers the way in which dominant social and legal practices may be informed by the unstated assumptions of the majority. It recognizes that these unstated assumptions, against which those who are different are often judged, simply serve to reinforce dominant practices, and endeavour to assimilate those who are different, into these dominant practices. In so doing, it recognizes that the protection of cultural minorities may require that these groups be treated in a manner that is not set by these dominant norms. It allows for a recognition of the validity of

---

[40] Martha Minow has explored the dilemmas of difference presented by a notion of equality as sameness. See Martha Minow, *Making all the Difference*, (1990).

cultural, religious and/or other differences, and opens the possibility that these differences need to be recognized and respected in law. At the same time, a substantive model of equality does not provide a formula which insists that minorities must always be treated differently. There will be contexts in which it would be quite inappropriate to treat minorities differently (such as the right to vote), and other contexts where it might be necessary (such as the right to worship on their own holy day). It simply creates the *possibility* that difference might be relevant, and directs attention to the *possibility* of systemic discrimination in dominant social and legal practices. In so doing, it challenges the pure majoritarianism of a formal approach to equality, by creating a legally principled defence for the protection of the rights of cultural minorities.[41]

A revisioning of equality along these lines will in turn allow for a re-examination of the meaning of equally respecting all religions, of ensuring that freedom of religion is equally guaranteed to all individuals and communities. Equal *respect* for all religions need not be taken to imply the equal *treatment* of all religions. Rather, a substantive approach would direct attention to the unstated norms implicit in the demand for equal treatment, that is, that minorities should be judged and treated in accordance with the norms of the majority. It would consider

[41] The substantive approach to equality has made some inroads into Indian legal and political discourse, as well as within the more specific discourse of Indian constitutional doctrine. On the one hand, Article 14 equality guarantees continue to be interpreted through the doctrine of reasonable classification that includes the similarly situated test within it. But, the case law around Article 15 prohibiting discrimination, and Article 16 promoting equality of opportunity within employment has recognized the need for 'preferential treatment' and 'compensatory discrimination' for disadvantaged groups. For a more detailed discussion of these approaches within Indian constitutional law, see Kapur and Cossman, (1993).

whether these norms are appropriate ones with which to judge cultural minorities, or whether the protection of the rights of cultural minorities requires that their differences be taken into account. Equally respecting cultural minorities thus means respecting their differences, and a substantive model would allow for these differences to be respected within the constitutional mandate of equality.

This model of equality could provide, for example, a principled basis on which to defend Article 30 of the Constitution, so consistently under attack by the Hindu Right. Article 30 provides that 'all minorities, whether based on religion or language, shall have the right to establish and administer educational institutions of their choice'.[42] A formal model of equality would have a difficult time providing a principled defence of this Article, but rather, could only explain it as an exception to the insistence of equal treatment. Indeed, the Hindu Right simply deploys this formal model in its attack. According to the BJP, Article 30 is a stark example of discrimination in favour of minorities, of special treatment and appeasement in violation of the constitutional principle of equality. In contrast, a substantive model of equality can defend Article 30 as part of, not an exception to, that principle. It would not blindly accept any and all differential treatment as constitutionally acceptable, but rather, would begin with an inquiry into the justification for this treatment. It would consider the importance of education for cultural minorities, such as the significance of educating their children in their own cultural traditions. It would consider the importance for cultural minorities of the right 'to conserve

---

[42] Article 30(1), Constitution of India. Article 30(2) further provides that 'The State shall not, in granting aid to educational institutions, discriminate against any educational institution on the ground that it is under the management of a minority, whether based on religion or language.'

its language, script and culture', and the centrality of educational institutions in such a pursuit. It might consider the likelihood of this kind of education in majority-run educational institutions, thus interrogating the possibility of systemic discrimination in dominant institutions. Further, it might consider the historically and socially disadvantaged position of these cultural minorities, and their lack of access to a range of social goods and services, including education. This substantive model of equality would then consider the importance of allowing these disadvantaged communities to control their own educational institutions as a way of ensuring more universal access to education for children from these communities. This substantive model of equality would not stumble over the mere fact of differential treatment. Rather, as long as that differential treatment was related to overcoming disadvantage and promoting substantive equality, it would be considered as an important component of the constitutional mandate of equality.

As we have argued elsewhere, although much Supreme Court jurisprudence follows a more formal model of equality, there is at least some case law that supports a more substantive model of equality.[43] Significantly, there is at least some case law that specifically supports this substantive model of equality in the context of the rights of cultural minorities. The Supreme Court has recognized the importance of Article 30 in promoting the real or substantive equality of minorities. In *St. Xavier's College v. State of Gujarat*, Justice Khanna stated:

Special rights for minorities were designed not to create inequality. Their real effect was to bring about equality by ensuring the preservation of the minority institutions and by guaranteeing to the minorities autonomy in the matter of the administration of those

---

[43] Kapur and Cossman, (1993), Introduction, n. 1.

institutions. The differential treatment for the minorities by giving them special rights, ensures that the ideal of equality may not be reduced to a mere abstract ideal but should become a living reality and result in true, genuine equality, an equality not merely in theory but also in fact.[44]

This recognition of the importance of minority rights, within a more substantive understanding of equality will be crucial in challenging the majoritarianism of the Hindu Right's approach to secularism. The courts can continue to build on the legacy of cases such as St. Xavier's College, and insist that real equality for cultural minorities must not be equated with sameness. In considering the scope and meaning of secularism within the Indian constitution, the courts can and should bring this understanding of substantive equality to their interpretations of 'equal respect for all religions.'

But challenging the formal understanding of equality that informs the Hindu Right's approach to secularism is a formidable task, because it is precisely this understanding of equality that has increasingly come to capture the popular imagination. The idea of equal treatment for all has increasingly taken on the aura of a truth claim; it has become a part of the collective common sense. Many of the advances made in equality theory— of recognizing the importance of differential treatment to address disadvantage and promote equality—have been met with a conservative backlash, which has attempted to recapture the terrain of equality, and limit its interpretative possibilities by insisting on 'equal treatment' as a self-evident truth. Not unlike the conservative assault on affirmative action in the United States, the Hindu Right along with other conservative forces in India have led the charge on 'special treatment' and 'appease-ment', endeavouring to regain the terrain lost in the discursive

[44] AIR 1974 SC 1389, p. 1415.

struggle over the meaning of equality. The success of its offensive may lie in the charming simplicity of the idea—after all, isn't equality all about treating people equally? The Hindu Right can simply appeal to this tautological reasoning, and insist that differential treatment ('appeasement') is then a violation of the constitutional mandate to treat people equally. It is a powerful discursive move that appears to have become increasingly difficult to counter in the public imagination. But it is precisely this powerful discursive move that *must* be countered if secularism is to be reappropriated from the Hindu Right, and revisioned in accordance with a more democratic political project.

FREEDOM OF RELIGION

Secondly, a revisioning of secularism requires the recuperation of the principle of freedom of religion. The importance of freedom of religion, as guaranteed in Articles 25 and 26 of the Constitution, needs to be reaffirmed and disarticulated from the majoritarian tendencies that have crept into this principle. Interestingly, it is in relation to freedom of religion that the Hindu Right's claim to secularism is weakest. In its discourse, freedom of religion is rarely specifically articulated as a political norm. Rather, as we argue, it speaks only of an individualized right to worship. The Hindu Right does not recognize the particular importance of the right to freedom of religion for religious minorities; it does not recognize that it is the religious beliefs and practices of these minorities that are most vulnerable; and it does not recognize that for these religious minorities, the right to freedom of religion is not simply a question of individual worship, but of their collective identity and cultural survival.

The recuperation of the principle of freedom of religion might begin, then, with a recognition that the principle must mean more than an *individual* right to *worship*. A substantive notion of freedom of religion must recognize that religious identity is necessarily constituted in and through a broader community. It must recognize that for religious minorities, there is more at stake than their individual right to worship. There is the matter of their collective survival—their right to practise their religion collectively, to educate their children according to their own beliefs, to attend public places of worship, to run their own religious institutions free from intervention. It is important to re-emphasize that freedom of religion is not simply an individual, but also a collective right, that is, it includes the rights of individuals and their religious organizations and associations to collectively pursue their religious beliefs.[45]

But to insist on such a vision is to do little more than insist on the rights that are already recognized and articulated within the Indian Constitution. Article 25 of the Constitution guarantees to all persons 'freedom of conscience and the right to freely profess, practice and propagate' their religion. Article 26 further guarantees 'to every religious denomination or any section thereof' certain collective rights of religion, including establishing and maintaining institutions for religious and charitable purposes, managing its own affairs in matters of religion,

[45] Smith, (1964), chapter 4, n. 7, has observed both the individual and collective dimensions to freedom of religion. On the individual dimension, he writes, 'Freedom of religion means that the individual is free to consider and discuss with others the relative claims of differing religions, and to come to his own decision without any interference from the state. He is free to reject them all. If he decides to embrace one religion, he has freedom to follow its teachings, participate in its worship and other activities, propagate its doctrines and hold office in its organizations' (p. 117). On the collective dimension, he writes, 'The collective aspect of this right is the freedom of two or more individuals to associate for religious purposes and to form permanent organizations to carry out these purposes' (p. 5).

owning, acquiring and administering property.[46] These constitutional guarantees clearly contemplate both individual and
collective rights to freedom of religion, that extend well beyond
the limited right to worship.

But, the problem with the Hindu Right's weak conception
of freedom of religion is not only its individualized nature.
Rather, in the discourse of the Hindu Right, freedom of religion
is envisioned entirely from the perspective of the majority
community, that is, in Hinduism, it is an individual right to
pursue one's own particular form of worship, based on the
Hindu belief in multiple and equally valid forms of worship.
It is then also a religious conception of freedom of religion, that
is, a conception of freedom of religion that is derived from the
principles of Hinduism. Indeed, it is then this religious conception of the freedom of religion that underlies the emphasis on
the individualized nature of the right. A recuperation of the
principle freedom of religion then must also challenge these
majoritarian and religious moorings of the principle within the
discourse of the Hindu Right.

Significantly, the Hindu Right is not alone in this majoritarian
approach to freedom of religion. Rather, there are examples

---

[46] The cases dealing with Articles 25 and 26 have focused largely around
delineating the legitimate sphere of State intervention in religion. Article 25
guarantees are subject to public order, health and morality. Article 25(2)
provides that the state is entitled to regulate and restrict 'any economic,
financial, political or other secular activity which may be associated with
religious practice' (25(2)(a)), and entitled to make laws for 'social welfare and
reform' (25(2)(b)). Article 26 guarantees are similarly subject to public order,
morality and health. The case law has attempted to further articulate the
grounds on which the state intervention contemplated by these articles is
justified. The Courts have held that the State is permitted to intervene to
regulate the secular activities of religious endowments. However, decisions
have tended to treat Article 26 as independent from Article 25, thus increasing
the scope of religion and the activities that are considered integral to a religion.

running through Supreme Court jurisprudence in which the unstated norm of the Hindu majority is all too evident. For example, Article 25 includes the right to propagate religion. This right was extensively debated in the Constituent Assembly, and included in the recognition of the fact that the propagation of religion is important in both Islam and Christianity. However, when considering whether Article 25 includes the right to proselytize, the Supreme Court placed restrictions on the right to propagate one's religion. In *Rev. Stainislaus v. State of Madhya Pradesh*, the Supreme Court held that Article 25 did not include a right to proselytize:

Article 25(1) guarantees 'freedom of conscience' to every citizen, and not merely to the followers of one particular religion, and that, in turn, postulates that there is no fundamental right to convert another person to one's own religion because if a person purposely undertakes the conversion of another person to his religion, as distinguished from his effort to transmit or spread the tenets of his religion, that would impinge on the 'freedom of conscience' guaranteed to all the citizens of the country alike.[47]

The Court in this case drew a dubious distinction between spreading the tenets of one's religion (propagating) and conversions (proselytizing)—a distinction that makes little sense to the religions of Islam and Christianity. Rather, it is a distinction that only makes sense from the unstated norm of the Hindu majority, which includes neither proselytizing nor conversions, and which sees itself as the target of the proselytizing of Islam and Christianity. The Supreme Court has interpreted the right to propagate not from the perspective of its importance to religious minorities, but rather, from the perspective of the right of the majority community to be free from interference with its religious practices, and it used a formal understanding of

[47] AIR 1977 SC 908, p. 911.

equality, emphasizing the equal treatment of all citizens, to support this conclusion.[48] In so doing, the Court failed to recognize the particular importance of the practice for religious minorities, emphasizing instead the importance that all citizens are equally free from religious interference. Since conversions were seen to interfere with the freedom of conscience of (Hindu) citizens, then the very practice that is so crucial to the religious beliefs of the Christian minority, was found to be outside the protection of freedom of religion.

A second example of the way in which the unstated norm of the majority has slipped into Supreme Court jurisprudence can be seen in some of the Court's discussions of the meaning of religion. In the case of *A. S. Narayana v. State of Andhra Pradesh*, Justice Hansaria briefly considered the meaning of religion as included and protected in Articles 25 and 26 of the Constitution.[49] In his view, the word 'religion' in these Articles is used 'in the sense conveyed by Dharma'.[50] He notes that although religion and dharma are often used interchangeably, the two terms are actually distinct. Citing Swami Rama, Justice Hansaria suggests that religion 'is comprised of rituals, customs and dogmas as surviving on the basis of fear and blind faith'. Dharma on the other hand 'encapsulates those great laws and disciplines that uphold, sustain and ultimately lead humanity to

---

[48] This conclusion must also be seen in the light of the significance of conversions in the politics of the Hindu Right. As we have discussed above, the mere fact that Islam and Christianity do proselytize is used by the Hindu Right as evidence of the intolerance of these religions, that is, that these religions do not equally respect other religions. The Hindu Right is unrelenting in its attack on the practice of conversions, often arguing that the practice particularly as conducted by the Christian community is fraudulent and coercive.

[49] AIR 1996 SC 1765.

[50] Ibid., p. 1805.

sublime heights of worldly and spiritual glory. Dharma shines in the form of truth, non-violence, love, compassion, forbearance, forgiveness and mutual sharing'.[51] The concept of dharma that Justice Hansaria concludes is the true meaning of the word 'religion' in Articles 25 and 26 is a concept entirely derived from Hinduism: he cites from the Rig Veda, the Mahabharata, Swami Vivekananda and Swami Rama. Certainly these, among other important Hindu texts and scholars, are the appropriate sources for a discussion of the concept of dharma within Hinduism. However, it is rather more controversial to suggest that these (and these alone) are the appropriate sources for an understanding of the meaning of religion contained in the Constitution, particularly for those very Articles that are intended to protect the rights of religious minorities. The opinion is an example of the ways in which the unstated norm of the Hindu majority can slip into judicial considerations of the meaning of religion, in subtle and not so subtle ways.[52]

We are not suggesting that either of these two decisions is representative of more general trends in Supreme Court jurisprudence on freedom of religion. Rather, we present them here simply as examples of the ways in which the unstated norms can, and sometimes do, slip into judicial reasoning. If the courts are to play a role in reversing the trends of Hindu majoritarianism, and promoting a democratic secularism, it will be essential to

[51] Ibid., p. 1807.

[52] Justice Hansaria's decision in the case was a brief concurring decision. But the majority decision—an extensive discussion of the meaning of religion was equally guilty, if not more so, of this deployment of the unstated Hindu norm in the discussion of the meaning of religion—admittedly, the case did involve a Hindu institution, and it might have been quite appropriate for the Court to focus its discussion on the meaning of religion within Hinduism. But the Court did not do so, preferring instead to wax eloquently on the true meaning of religion more generally, while drawing almost entirely on Hindu sources.

guard against the incursions of such majoritarianism in its own decisions. The courts must be vigilant in ensuring that the unstated norms of the Hindu majority do not inadvertently slip into legal and constitutional discourse in general. But this vigilance is all the more crucial in the context of interpreting those very articles of the Constitution that are intended to protect and promote the rights of minorities. It will be important to guard against any judicial limitations on the constitutional guarantees to freedom of religion. The courts must struggle to disarticulate their own understanding of freedom of religion from the unstated norms of the majority, and recognize the fundamental importance of freedom of religion from the point of view of religious minorities.

But again the problem is not one of legal discourse alone. It is rather a broader political problem in which the Hindu Right is increasingly capturing the popular imagination. It is, after all, in relation to freedom of religion, and the protection of religious minorities that the Hindu Right has been demanding constitutional amendments.[53] It may not be enough to re-assert the importance of the protection of freedom of religion within the Constitution, when the Hindu Right is challenging the very

---

[53] For example, the BJP has long demanded the reform of Article 30 of the Constitution. Article 30(1) provides that 'All minorities, whether based on religion or language, shall have the right to establish and administer educational institutions of their choice.' Article 30(2) prohibits the State from discriminating against any educational institution in granting aid to educational institutions 'on the ground that it is under the management of a minority, whether based on religion or language.' According to the BJP, Article 30 is part of a general policy of appeasement of the minorities. In its most recent 1998 Election Manifesto, the BJP states that its commitments include 'Amend(ing) Article 30 of the Constitution suitably to remove any scope of discrimination against any religious community in matters of education' (p. 36).

legitimacy of that protection with increasing efficacy. Defending the rights of religious minorities to freedom of religion will require challenging the multiple discourses through which the Hindu Right is attacking these minorities. While freedom of religion may be the weak link in the Hindu Right's rhetorical chain, it is a link that is reinforced by the Hindu Right's approach to the other dimensions of secularism, that is, equality and toleration. The inroads of the Hindu Right have been in relation to *these* concepts, and it is these concepts that are increasingly limiting the common sense conception of the appropriate scope and content of freedom of religion. It is in its understanding of formal equality that any recognition of religious differences—differences that need to be recognized in accordance with the constitutional requirement of freedom of religion—becomes a violation of the Constitutional guarantee of equality. Similarly, as we discuss in more detail below, it is through its understanding of Hinduism as the only tolerant religion that the right of religious minorities to profess and propagate their 'intolerant' religions is cast as a violation of the freedom of religion. The site of contestation, then, seems to be less one over freedom of religion than over equality and toleration, that is, the Hindu Right's discourse of freedom of religion seems to be almost entirely derivative from its conceptions of equality and toleration. This is not to suggest that the struggle over freedom of religion in the effort to revitalize and redemocratize secularism will be easy, or can afford to be ignored. It is only to suggest that freedom of religion does not itself seem to be a central and independent component of the Hindu Right's discourse.

Strategically, then, it will be important to reveal the Hindu Right's real position on freedom of religion, namely, that it does not agree with the constitutional guarantees of the individual and collective right to freely practise, profess and propagate religion. A revitalized conception of freedom of religion will require attention to the importance of freedom of religion from the perspective of the minority communities—to both the rights of individuals within those communities to practise, profess and propagate their religion, as well as the collective right of those communities to their religious identity and cultural survival. In conjunction with a substantive model of equality, a substantive and democratic vision of freedom of religion will require a recognition of the need to accommodate religious difference— that protecting the rights of religious minorities will require that their differences be taken into account.[54] And a revisioned conception of freedom of religion must not be based on a specifically religious (and Hindu) approach, which in our view is unable to accommodate those religious minorities who do not agree that there are multiple forms of worship and paths to god.

[54] The need for state recognition and accommodation of religious difference is perhaps easier in the Indian context than in the American, since there is no equivalent of the anti-Establishment clause in the Indian constitutional protection of freedom of religion. Indian case law has explicitly recognized that the state may intervene in the religions, in certain specific contexts. State intervention in religion is specifically contemplated by the very articles that guarantee freedom of religion, and a major focus of the case law under Articles 25 and 26 has been delineating the legitimate scope of state intervention. Indeed, it is important to recall that it is this constitutional legitimacy of state intervention in religion that distinguishes Indian secularism from American concepts of secularism. See chapter 4, notes 13–15; see also Smith (1964) chapter 4, n. 7). The accommodation of religious difference thus would not run into the same problems of violating the prohibition on any state recognition of religion. Although many difficult dilemmas of determining when state intervention in religion is justifiable continue to plague Indian constitutional law, the constitutional framework is nevertheless one which would allow for a substantive approach to the recognition of group difference.

Rather, freedom of religion will have to be based on a political commitment to religious plurality and diversity, that is capable of recognizing that different religions have different opinions on the question of religious belief and practice. A democratic revisioning of freedom of religion thus requires that it be released from its individual, religious and majoritarian moorings. The unstated norms of the majority must be displaced in favour of explicitly articulated democratic norms that recognize the importance of minority rights.

TOLERATION

Finally, the principle of toleration—secularism's third principle—must also be democratized. The point of departure for such a process must be the disarticulation of toleration from its majoritarian and explicitly religious moorings. Dominant discourses of secularism have emphasized that the principle of toleration is derived from the cultural traditions of Indian society—cultural traditions that more often than not are equated with Hindu traditions, and Hinduism. Although this majoritarian and religious basis of toleration has been made most explicit in the discourse of the Hindu Right, it is also apparent in the constitutional discourse of secularism. The very reason that Indian secularism is said to be different than the western lies in this concept of toleration, and the claim that historically, Indian society in general, and Hinduism in particular, has been tolerant of other religions. The advocates of Indian secularism as the equal respect for all religions have time and again emphasized this historical and cultural grounding. The Hindu Right has simply taken up this grounding, and developed it in its own distinctive and aggressively nationalistic direction.

Toleration has been cast as the characteristic of the majority Hindu community. If the concept of toleration is to be democratized, it must be delinked from these majoritarian and religious foundations. However, to do so would be to risk undermining the very foundation of the distinctive nature of Indian secularism. We thus encounter a troubling paradox: the majoritarian and religious character of toleration is precisely the characteristic that gives Indian secularism its distinctive nature. Indeed, this paradox gives credence to Upadhyaya's position that it is this concept of secularism that has created the problems of majoritarianism. One way out might then be to abandon this concept of secularism in favour of one that returns to the principle of neutrality. But, as we have argued, it is the dominant discourse of secularism that offers the most political promise. The dilemma then is how to escape from this paradox, without abandoning the dominant discourse of secularism as equal respect for all religions?

Rather than disarticulating toleration from its religious moorings altogether, a second option might be to pluralize the cultural and religious traditions on which it is based. Rather than emphasizing the exclusivity of Hinduism as a tolerant religion, this pluralizing strategy would search for toleration's historical roots in the multiplicity of India's religious traditions. This pluralizing strategy is often sanctioned in dominant discourses and institutions. For example, it can be seen in a number of court decisions of secularism, where famous speeches are cited that point to the tradition of toleration in India's rich, multi-religious past. But, in our view, there are many risks associated with such a religious basis of toleration.

First, despite its best intentions, this pluralizing strategy always runs the risk of majoritarianism. In the Ayodhya decision,[55] for example the Court attempts to tell a story of

---

[55] *M. Ismail Faruqui v. Union of India*, Preface, n. 7. In this case, the constitutionality of the Acquisition of Certain Land at Ayodhya Act (1993)

India's rich tapestry of toleration, by weaving together a pastiche of citations from famous speeches and decisions that in turn cite other famous work and speeches. But this pastiche does not amount to a particularly rigorous historical methodology. Indeed, these somewhat questionable historical reconstructions bear more than a passing resemblance to Nandy's nostalgic idealism. Moreover, despite the Court's efforts at presenting a pluralized tradition of toleration, a closer examination of these passages reveals that the only religious scripture that is cited is Hindu: the Yajurveda, the Atharva Veda, the Rig Veda. While one of the quotes makes reference to the Quran, there are no similar quotations from it. Admittedly, the Court might be on shaky ground quoting from the Quran. Indeed, there have been instances where the Court did dare to interpret the Quran that has landed it in more than a little controversy.[56] But given that the Court does go on to discuss the relevance of a mosque in the practice of Islam,[57] it is difficult to give too much weight to its desire to avoid controversy by not (mis)interpreting Islamic scriptures and practice. Rather, the failure to cite any non-Hindu scripture reveals, once again, the

---

was challenged. Justice Verma, writing for the majority of the Court (Chief Justice Venkatachaliah and Justice Ray concurring) upheld the constitutionality of the Act, rejecting inter alia arguments that the Act was in any way slanted towards Hindus, or discriminating against Muslims. Justice Bharucha, (Justice Ahmadi concurring), in a minority decision, concluded that the Act was slanted in favour of the Hindus, and did therefore offend the basic principle of secularism.

[56] At least part of the controversy surrounding the Shah Bano decision had to do with the fact that the Supreme Court had interpreted the Quran.

[57] The Court concluded 'A mosque is not an essential part of the practice of the religion of Islam and Namaz (prayer) by Muslims can be offered anywhere, even in the open. Accordingly, its acquisition is not prohibited by the provisions in the Constitution of India' n. 55 above, para 85).

extent to which the unstated norm of the majority slips into judicial discourse.[58]

The response to this critique may be that it is not the strategy itself of pluralizing India's cultural traditions that is at fault, but rather, the Court's failure to do so. In the name of multiple traditions, the unstated norm of the majority remains at the centre. Again, the problem comes down to one of majoritarianism. Accordingly, it might be argued that this unstated norm should be decentred, and the historical basis of the Indian tradition of toleration truly pluralized. But beyond this risk of majoritarianism, there are a number of other limitations with a religious basis of toleration. It is an approach that begins to approximate the strategy advocated by Nandy, for a 'tolerance that is religious', and therefore, a tolerance that is located 'outside the ideological grid of modernity'.[59] It therefore bears similar problems of a return to pre-modern forms, uncontaminated by India's encounter with colonialism and modernity. There are risks of nostalgic idealism and cultural essentialism—of searching for the elusive authenticity of religious and cultural traditions, of assuming that those traditions can be discovered rather than constructed and negotiated, and of reconstructing those traditions as static, immutable, and monolithic.[60]

---

[58] In stark contrast to the majority, the minority decision in the Ayodhya case did not deploy a religious conception of toleration, but rather based its conception of secularism briefly, but firmly, within the Constitution. See n. 55 above, para 144.

[59] Nandy, op. cit. (1985, 1998), chapter 5, n. 2.

[60] On this critique of cultural essentialism, see Stuart Hall 'Cultural Identity and Cinematic Representation' in Baker et. al., (eds), Black British Cultural Studies: A Reader, (1996) p. 210. See also Ratna Kapur, 'A Love Song to Our Mongrel Selves: Hybridity, Sexuality and the Law', Social and Legal Studies (forthcoming, 1999).

Moreover, we are concerned that a religious conception of toleration would be limited to religious toleration. By this we mean that a religious conception of toleration is based on the idea that there are different forms of worship and religious practice that ultimately all lead to the same place. It is based on the idea that underneath the surface manifestations of these different religious beliefs, practices and forms of worship, is a common religiosity. This religious toleration is based very much on religion itself—on recognizing the legitimacy of different religions. This conception of toleration may appear to be extremely useful in the context of a religious pluralistic society, particularly one characterized by an increasing erosion of respect for religious minorities, as is the case in contemporary India. But it is not entirely uncontroversial. Donald Eugene Smith observed that the emphasis on religious and specifically Hindu toleration may actually be disputed by minority communities. He argued:

While the social attitude of tolerance is an unmixed asset, the proposition that all religions are equally true and ultimately the same has significant limitations as a theoretical foundation for the secular state... The theory will not be acceptable to those Muslims, Christians. and others who believe that there are elements of ultimate uniqueness in their respective faiths. Any theory which cannot be broadly shared by the members of the minority community is of limited usefulness.[61]

Moreover, it is a concept of toleration that does not extend beyond a toleration of religious difference. This religious toleration could not address the importance of tolerating those who think, act and live differently, if those differences were based on something other than religion. It would not be applicable in the context of political differences or moral differences, where toleration may be called for. For example,

[61] Smith, (1964), chapter 4, n. 7, p. 150.

homosexuality and sexual difference is an issue around which there is a high degree of controversy. In the U.S., and elsewhere, there are conservative political movements that not only do not tolerate homosexuals, but which strive at eliminating homosexuality altogether. Similarly, one wonders whether other sexually different groups would be tolerated in India. For example, would the *hijra*, who expounds the theory of religious toleration to the lost twin in Mani Ratnam's film, *Bombay*, that all religions lead to one God/truth, in turn be accommodated within a concept of toleration based on religiosity? Despite the toleration of hijras in public spaces and popular culture, a religious conception of toleration may not support an argument for toleration towards such sexual sub-groups. Similarly, a religious conception of toleration would unlikely be up to the task of promoting tolerance towards racial, rather than religious minorities. Nor would a religious conception of toleration be up to the task of accommodating those of different political persuasions, like communists or pacifists. A principle of toleration appropriate for our times must be one that is up to the challenge of not only promoting respect of difference along religious lines, but also along a range of other fault lines.

In our view, then, it would be preferable to develop an approach to toleration that is capable of accommodating a fuller range of conflicts and cleavages. For all these reasons, we return to the idea of disarticulating toleration from its religious and majoritarian moorings. Rather than basing toleration in religion, we prefer a political conception of toleration. We are more comfortable, then, with Chatterjee's effort at refashioning a political (rather than Nandy's religious) conception of toleration—one that acknowledges the irreversible mark that modernity has made on our times, and recognizes that a commitment to living together across our differences will have to be carved out of this modernity, not in opposition to it.[62] In terms of legal and political discourse, toleration would no longer need to be derived from ancient sources, but rather, approached as a constitutional value in its own right. This political norm would begin from the most basic premise of toleration—accepting people and their practices despite our disagreements and disapproval. It means not only accepting differences, but accepting those differences that at some level we find unacceptable. It is a conception of toleration then, that goes beyond the mere acceptance of different forms of worship. It is a normative commitment to accepting a broad range of differences in beliefs, practices and ways of being, made necessary by the pluralistic and fragmented world in which we live.[63]

Our preference for a political conception of toleration will no doubt be met with opposition from some quarters. In arguing that the basis for toleration should be political rather than religious, are we not simply showing our 'secular' (read anti-religious) bias, and attempting to displace the very recognition of religion that is said to lie at the root of the distinctive nature of Indian secularism? Are we not reintroducing the very distinction that the Indian conception of secularism is intended to escape, that is, the separation of religion and politics? At the level of principle, perhaps we are guilty of reintroducing this distinction. But, at a more pragmatic level, it is not our intention to banish a reliance on religious conceptions of toleration altogether. To the extent that a reliance on this religious toleration may assist in challenging the rising tides of majoritarianism, and recreating a public space which respects the rights of those who

[62] Although we continue to disagree with Chatterjee, in so far as we believe that this reconfiguring of toleration can occur within secularism.

[63] For an argument on the value of toleration, see T. M. Scanlon, 'The Difficulty of Tolerance' in Bhargava, ed., chapter 3, n. 5.

are different, it should be used in day-to-day struggles for recuperating a democratic vision of toleration.[64]

Nor are we suggesting that religious imagery must be abandoned in the effort to promote the value of toleration. Writing in response to the appropriation of secular language and idioms by communalists, Rustom Bharucha has argued that this appropriation, though obviously troubling, should not lead to an abandonment of Hindu icons and imagery. 'It should be acknowledged that while "Hindu" imagery may be "majoritarian"...this cannot justify the erasure of "Hindu" sources, even if this were possible. For, this erasure would be a censorship in its own right, revealing an intolerance of those cultural resources that may be very precious to the majority of one's own colleagues.'[65] To the extent that this imagery continues to have real meaning in people's lives, those committed to a vision of democratic secularism abandon it at their own peril. Perhaps we need not exclude the possibility of a religious conception of toleration from the secular equation altogether, but rather need, to point out at a principled level its risks and limitations, to suggest that a religious conception of toleration is insufficient, and to argue in favour of a broader, political conception.

Finally, it is important to emphasize that our focus is on the legal and constitutional discourse of secularism, and that it is specifically in relation to this legal and constitutional discourse

[64] The question that remains unanswered for us, however, is the extent to which such a religious conception of toleration *can* be used in challenging majoritarianism. Our anxiety around this religious conception of toleration continues to be the extent to which it appears to have been, in practice, deeply majoritarian. We do not want to close the door on a potentially useful resource for promoting toleration, but we remain unconvinced of its ability to do so.

[65] Rustom Bharucha, 'In the Name of the Secular: Cultural Interactions and Interventions', *EPW* (November 5, 1994), p. 2925.

that we believe it will be important for the courts to disentangle toleration from its religious and majoritarian basis. While there may be a strategic place for a religious conception of toleration in the public sphere and popular culture, we do not believe that it has a place in law. Rather, it is important, in the discursive struggles in the legal arena, to develop a political conception of toleration in which this basic principle of secularism is valued in its own right. When the Supreme Court has attempted to base its conception of toleration in religion (as in the *Ayodhya* decision), it has failed to adequately pluralize this toleration, resting instead on the unstated norms of the majority. But when the Court has based its conception of secularism and in turn, toleration on the Constitution itself (as in the *Bommai* case), it has been on much stronger ground.[66] The courts should not feel compelled to search ancient texts to legitimatize the rightful place of toleration in the Indian constitution, but rather, should confidently assert toleration as its own constitutional value. They should play to their strengths—strengths which lie in neither history nor ancient scriptures—but in legal precedent and values. Toleration should become such a legal value in its own right.

Beyond this question of the normative basis of toleration, it will also be important to more specifically articulate the requirements of an approach to toleration. First, it is necessary to

---

[66] It is at least worth observing that these two decisions, along with the *Hindutva* cases, were all decided within less than a year of each other. The high water-mark in the Supreme Court's protection of secularism in *Bommai* (11.3.94), and the low water-marks of both the *Ayodhya* (24.10.1994) and the *Hindutva* (11.12.1995) decisions were all decided in the 1994 and 1995 Supreme Court terms. It is also noteworthy that the majority decision in the *Ayodhya* case and the decision of the Court in the *Hindutva* case were both written by Justice Verma. And in the *Bommai* case, Justice Verma was one of only two judges who did not pass comment in any way on the importance of secularism in the Indian Constitution.

consider the meaning of toleration, and the kind of state action that it mandates. As we have already mentioned, toleration is generally said to require that we accept people and their practices, even when we strongly disagree with and disapprove of them.[67] But this statement of principle leaves many difficult questions unanswered. What kind of state action does this acceptance require? Does tolerating subgroups involve non-intervention in their affairs? Or does it require a more substantive accommodation of group differences? Martha Minow has explored this question, along with many other dilemmas that toleration presents to the accommodation of subgroups and cultural minorities.[68] She argues that if toleration simply involves non-intervention in the views and practices of the subgroup, it will fail to adequately respect the subgroup. According to Minow, 'mere non-interference' cannot convey:

The ideas captured by tolerance, especially where non–interference occurs within a context in which the viewpoint or practice does not conform to the majority practices. The majority may stigmatize, deride, or chill the adoption of minority group viewpoints or practices. The majority may undermine the conditions subgroups need to preserve in order to flourish. Apparently equal policies that nonetheless fail to accommodate the differences of a minority culture edge toward intolerance if those policies make expression or maintenance of the minority culture's views or practices difficult or costly to members of that group.[69]

In her view, the protection of cultural minorities requires more than toleration—it requires a respect for cultural diversity, which she defines as 'a more active demand than toleration, for it may call for accommodation of subgroup practices and, therefore, changes in dominant institutions'.

[67] See Scanlon, in Bhargava (ed.), chapter 3, n. 5.
[68] Martha Minow, 'Putting Up and Putting Down: Tolerance Reconsidered', *Osgoode Hall Law Journal*, 28, (1990), p. 409.
[69] Ibid., pp 422–3.

Minow's critique points out the ways in which the liberal value of toleration has been extended by, and measured according to, dominant social groups and dominant social norms. The Hindu Right's unapologetically majoritarian approach to toleration can be seen within this framework. The Hindu Right has promoted a vision of toleration which is based explicitly on dominant social groups and norms. Its vision that only Hindus can be truly tolerant is but an extreme example of the liberal dilemma of toleration, which locates toleration within dominant communities, and which extends toleration to others only to the extent that those communities are seen to accept and practise a similar vision of it. One of the paradoxes of toleration, then, is that its location within dominant social groups and norms always runs the risk of undermining the very practices of subgroups that it purports to tolerate. Mere non-intervention may be inadequate to the task of accommodating the subgroup; indeed non-intervention perpetuates the very oppressive conditions that subgroups struggle against for their very survival. Yet, non-intervention may be all that stands in the way of the goal of assimilation. From the point of view of the cultural minorities that are under attack from the Hindu Right, even weak toleration as mere non-intervention may seem to be an increasingly attractive and elusive norm.

While the critique of toleration is an important one which helps complicate our inquiry, we are of the view that it remains politically and legally efficacious to retain it in the struggle for India's secular democracy. In a political environment characterized by increasing and violent intolerance, the principle of toleration is one well worth fighting for. It seems incontrovertible that toleration has been measured against dominant social norms, and in this respect, is a principle that seems to be inherently majoritarian. But this critique of the majoritarian nature of toleration is a long way from the kind of majoritarianism

we have identified in the Hindu Right's approach. In the context
of contemporary India, even the kind of weak toleration which
Minow and others have rightly critiqued is little in evidence,
and given the explicitly majoritarian and communalist approach
of the Hindu Right that only Hindus are tolerant, a liberal
notion of toleration would be a considerable advancement from
the point of view of cultural minorities.

At the same time, it is important to continue to wrestle
toleration away from its majoritarian moorings—from the
extreme majoritarianism of the Hindu Right to the more subtle
majoritarianism of liberal toleration. In our view, a democratized vision of toleration that accompanies a substantive vision
of equality is one that must include the kind of respect for
cultural diversity that Minow advocates. It is a vision of
toleration that requires more than a passive acceptance of
different points of view; that will require an active accommodation of sub-group practices, and that may at times require
changes in dominant institutions. It is a vision of toleration that,
alongside a substantive approach to equality, requires an explicit
recognition of group difference, and challenges dominant norms
as the appropriate norms against which to judge cultural
minorities.

A second recurring question that plagues the principle of
toleration is whether the principle is to be extended to groups
that do not themselves accept the liberal value, and do not
govern their own internal group affairs according to its dictates.
The question, in other words, involves when toleration should
be extended to sub-groups. Must sub-groups be tolerated that
do not accept toleration? The problem is one that again
highlights the extent to which toleration is measured against the
norms of the dominant community. It is the dominant community that holds the principle of toleration as supreme, and it is

this dominant community that has the power to decide if and when the practices of the subgroup are to be tolerated.[70]

Partha Chatterjee has explored this dilemma of toleration specifically within the context of India, and the assault on minority rights by the Hindu Right.[71] Beginning with a concern about liberal democratic theory's inability to accommodate the claim of collective rights of cultural groups,[72] Chatterjee refuses to give up on toleration, and instead tries to find a defensible argument for minority cultural rights in the given legal-political situation prevailing in India. His analysis attempts to reveal the extent to which the Indian state has failed to live up to the three basic principles of liberal democratic secularism—freedom of religion, equality, and separation of state and religion. As discussed above, Chatterjee then suggests that the problem of the rise of the Hindu Right and its assault on minorities should be refigured not as a problem of secularism, but as a problem of toleration. In so doing, he has initiated a process of rethinking the principle of toleration, arguing that the principle of respect for persons provides a moral basis for not only defending toleration but also respecting the rights of cultural groups.

Chatterjee engages with the specific requirements of toleration and sub-groups, including the dilemma of extending toleration to those groups that are 'intolerant towards [their]

[70] As Minow has argued, (above, n. 36) liberal notions of tolerance may thus appear to be disrespectful from the point of view of cultural minorities, who do not accept the liberal value of tolerance itself.

[71] Chatterjee, above, n. 13.

[72] Ibid. He argues that there is 'no viable way out of this problem within the given contours of liberal democratic theory which must define the relations between the relatively autonomous domains of state and civil society in terms always of individual rights. As has been noticed for many other species of emerging forms of non-western modernity, this is one more instance where the supposedly universal forms of the modern state turn out to be inadequate for the postcolonial world.' Ibid., p. 1773.

own members and show inadequate respect for persons.' And in engaging with this dilemma, he attempts to move beyond the typical liberal insistence on an individual right to exist. Chatterjee attempts to reconfigure the content of toleration, that is, to reframe the kind of treatment that the dominant community will have to extend to subgroups. He argues that toleration will have to involve more than the mere right to be different:

Equally important is the other half of the assertion: 'We have our own reasons for doing things the way we do'. This implies the existence of a field of reasons, of processes through which reasons can be exchanged and validated, even if such processes are open only to those who share the viewpoint of the group. The existence of this autonomous discursive field may only be implied and not activated, but the implication is a necessary part of the assertion of cultural autonomy as a matter of right.[73]

Chatterjee argues that the principle of toleration will require accepting 'that there will be political contexts where a group could insist on its right not to give reasons for doings things differently provided it explains itself adequately in its own chosen forum.'[74] Cultural minorities will need to ensure that procedures and processes exist through which they can 'publicly seek and obtain from its members consent for its practices insofar as those practices have regulative power over the members.'[75] It is, in effect, a call for some kind of internal

[73] Ibid.

[74] Ibid.

[75] Chatterjee elaborates: 'It is not necessary that there be a single uniform pattern of seeking consent that each group will be required to follow. But it is necessary, if toleration is to be demanded, that the processes satisfy the same condition of representativeness that is invoked when a legislative body elected under universal franchise is found unsuitable to act on matters concerning the religion of minority groups. In other words, even if a religious group declares that the validity of its practices can only be discussed and judged in its own forums, those institutions must have the same degree of publicity and

accountability or democracy that becomes the prerequisite for extending the principle of toleration, and in turn, for accommodating a cultural minority's right to do things differently.

His critique is a provocative one, which will no doubt be met with considerable opposition from those who fear that he is relinquishing too much autonomy to highly conservative, even orthodox, communities to manage their own affairs without sufficient concern for toleration within their own ranks. Some may fear that his suggestion for reconfiguring the problem of toleration is one that will ultimately cede all normative universality in favour of an extreme cultural relativism. On one hand, Chatterjee appears to be abandoning a commitment to the norms of universal citizenship, and arguing instead for a recognition of differences within communities. But, on the other hand, there are underlying universal norms informing his vision—namely, of democratic accountability, of respect for persons, of autonomy and self-representation. In his refashioned vision of toleration, it is the existence of some structures of accountability and democratic representation that operate as the prerequisite for the dominant community's willingness to extend toleration to the sub-group. The recognition of differences is thus premised on the cultural minority agreeing to abide by these basic normative commitments to some form of democratic accountability: its members must consent. Chatterjee is then, attempting to formulate a middle ground, 'a somewhere in between' universal principles and the recognition of difference.[76]

---

representativeness that is demanded of all public institutions having regulatory functions' (Ibid.).

[76] In some ways, Chatterjee can be seen to have simply shifted the nature of the problem, from one of toleration to one of accountability and democracy. In this way, he is not completely breaking out of the imposition of some normative framework on cultural minorities. But, by the same token,

But Chatterjee's middle ground for reconfiguring the problem of toleration leaves many questions unanswered, particularly in view of the legal or constitutional approach to toleration. It is difficult to imagine how, if at all, his propositions could be translated into the legal domain. For example, would courts accept the principle of a right not to give reasons, given that this legal arena is all about giving reasonable argument? Could or should courts be called upon to adjudicate issues such as whether cultural minorities have met the minimal requirement of internal accountability? Would we not expect to encounter precisely the same problem of majoritarianism? Further, in our view, Chatterjee may have prematurely abandoned the importance of the 'mere right to be different'—a right that is little in evidence in the discourse of the Hindu Right. Rather, it may be that there are still important strategic and interpretative possibilities in emphasizing this dimension of toleration, and revealing that the Hindu Right's assimilative agenda does not, in any substantive way, accept the right to be really different (rather, difference within their vision is religious difference within Hinduism, not outside of it, and certainly not non-religious difference). But, notwithstanding these limitations, Chatterjee's suggestions are worthy of engagement, in so far as they *attempt* to provide the basis for a principled defence of some degree of autonomy for cultural minorities, provided that those minorities abide by a basic degree of democratic accountability. The continued erosion of toleration at the hands of the Hindu Right makes the defence of the rights of cultural minorities an important political commitment, and we believe

---

we are of the view that the prerequisites of some form of representation, which, as Chatterjee suggests, may take very different social and political contexts into account, does seem to be the appropriate one within the context of a political project expressly committed to a democratic vision.

that critically engaging with Chatterjee's work (on the terrain of secularism rather than in opposition to it) may be helpful in refocusing attention on this political norm.

In our view, both Minow's and Chatterjee's efforts at refashioning the scope and content of toleration may be insightful in the effort to ground secularism within more democratic politics. In particular, their insistence on the importance of group rights and of the rights of cultural minorities to some degree of self-governance and self-determination is an important contribution towards redemocratizing the principles that inform Indian secularism. Further, underlying both Minow's and Chatterjee's work is a shared belief that the principle of respect for persons must be the basis for toleration, and which must serve as the arbiter in attempting to resolve the dilemmas that toleration continues to present. It is this principle of respect for persons that must inform efforts at resolving the questions of when to tolerate those who do not appear to hold toleration as a cherished value, or how to balance a commitment to universal norms with a respect for cultural difference.

Our discussion may appear to have come full circle, back to the principle of respect that is said to represent Indian secularism—equal *respect* for all religions. But the principle of respect that we are contemplating here is not one premised on simply respecting religions, but on respecting the individuals within those religions, and it is to be read within a political conception of toleration committed to accepting those that we disagree with. This political conception of toleration, informed by the principle of respect, may go some distance in challenging the majoritarian toleration of the Hindu Right. Their message that only Hindus are truly tolerant—since they alone do not proselytize—is not a message based on respect for people who belong to other religions. On the contrary, the sub-text is that these

other religions (read Islam and Christianity) are simply inferior
to Hinduism, and therefore, not equally deserving of respect.
The conception of toleration that we are articulating here may
help reveal this intolerance of the Hindu Right. If toleration
requires that we accept people and their practices, even when
we strongly disagree with and disapprove of them, then it does
not allow such a condemnation of religious minorities for their
practice of conversions. Even if one were to believe that this
practice was wrong, tolerance—at its most general level—
requires that these practices be accepted. Further, if toleration
requires respect for cultural diversity, for the members of the
cultural minority and their different ways of being and believing, then it does not allow a condemnation of the religious
practices of the cultural minorities, in the fashion of the Hindu
Right. Indeed, in their world, respect is a rather one-sided
affair—it is demanded of others, but rarely extended to them.

The principle of respect may also provide a defence against
those who fear that in recognizing cultural diversity, we are
headed down a road of cultural relativism, where even the most
intolerant practices must be tolerated. The principle of respect
can provide the prerequisite for the extension of toleration—that
only those communities who demonstrate respect towards their
members will qualify for toleration. As Chatterjee appears to
acknowledge, '[t]oleration is required by the principle of respect
for persons, but practices which fail to show respect for persons
need not be tolerated.'[77] At the same time, the principle of
respect is unlikely to resolve all the dilemmas presented by
toleration, since there will undoubtedly be very different
understandings of what respect requires. To promote respect as
the arbiter may be to simply shift the site of disagreement and

[77] Ibid.

contestation between majority and minority communities.[78] But the idea of respect for persons at least provides a minimum, universal normative commitment by which these continuing conflicts and dilemmas might be arbitrated.

To return, then, to the principle of equal toleration of all religions, a revisioning of toleration along the lines we have suggested will allow for an approach to secularism that does not preclude the recognition of group differences, but rather, begins with an affirmation of the importance of accommodating these differences. Equal toleration of all religions need not be taken to imply equal treatment. Nor need it imply that the practices and views of religious minorities be brought in line with those of the dominant community in order to qualify for toleration. Rather, following from, and in line with, the substantive vision of equality that we have advocated, equal toleration of all religions would recognize that differences can be accommodated and respected, including those differences which the majority community may disagree with or disapprove of. Equal tolera- tion would recognize the validity of different ways of being and of believing, and attempt to create the social space required to accommodate those differences.

[78] For example, there are sharp disagreements over the application of the principle of respect for women. Conservative movements, including the Hindu Right, espouse a deeply gendered notion of respect—of returning women to the position of respect that they once enjoyed in a past golden age; of honouring (and limiting) women in their roles as mothers and wives. By contrast, feminist arguments, at their most general level, would emphasize that respect requires ensuring women's full and equal participation in society, while eliminating the negative stereotypes that have operated as obstacles to such participation.

6

Conclusion

The Hindu Right has produced crude fantasies about Hinduism and Hindu history, fantasies that are nevertheless capturing much of the popular imagination. They are contriving a new belief system and structure that relies on neither historical truth nor evidence, but invention and fabrication. The entire struggle over Ayodhya is a struggle by the Right to signpost the spot where God was born. Their construction of the Hindu faith and religion is the very antithesis of plurality. Their version of what constitutes true belief is, to use the words of one of Rushdie's characters, 'bumkum'.

What bunkum, I swear', she expostulated. 'Point one: in a religion with a thousand and one gods they suddenly decide only one chap matters. Then what about Calcutta, for example, where they don't go for Ram? And Shiva-temples are no longer suitable places of worship? Too stupid. Point two: Hinduism has many holy books, not one, but suddenly it is all Ramayan, Ramayan. Then where is the Gita? Where are all the Puranas? How dare they twist everything in this way? Bloody joke. And point three: for Hindus there is no requirement for a collective act of worship, but without that how are these types going to collect their beloved mobs? So suddenly there is this invention of mass puja, and that is declared the only way to show true, class-A devotion. A single, martial deity, a single book, and mob rule: that is what they have made of Hindu culture, its many-headed beauty, its peace.[1]

It is the support that the Supreme Court has given to this fantastical rewriting by giving its seal of secular approval to the term 'Hindutva' that we believe is deeply troubling. While the BJP coalition government teeters on the brink of collapse, the mythology of the Hindu Right shows very few signs of collapse alongside it. For the power of the Hindu Right lies in the discursive and ideological realms, in the highly diffuse ways in which the Hindu religion, history and nation have been reinvented along the fault lines of Hindutva. In the wake of the *Hindutva* cases, the law itself has now become complicit in this rewriting.

There are certainly no easy answers in the ongoing struggle for secularism in Indian democracy, and the continuing ascendance of the Hindu Right, with its own distinctive claim to secularism, has only increased the stakes. We do not believe that the struggle for secularism will be exclusively a legal one. It will not be courts, or legal discourse alone, that will be the sites of contestation. But we do believe that law and legal discourse will be one important site of this broader discursive struggle, and that the courts will have a role in defending secularism from the corrosive influence of the Hindu Right. As we have attempted to argue, however, the Supreme Court is not fully living up to its role. Despite the Court's efforts in earlier decisions to defend a strong constitutional secularism, the *Hindutva* cases mark a decisive shift. The Supreme Court's decision has effectively legitimatized the Hindu Right's understanding of secularism,

---

[1] Salman Rushdie, *The Moor's Last Sigh*, (1995), p. 338.

and paradoxically, opened the door for its non-secular agenda. At the same time, it is important to acknowledge that the Supreme Court remains critical of the Hindu Right. Although we have argued that the *Hindutva* cases represent an important discursive victory for the Hindu Right, the victory is not an unequivocal one. Despite its vindication of the Hindu Right's vision of Hindutva, and its vision of secularism, the Court did in fact condemn, in no uncertain terms, the practices of several members of the Hindu Right, most notably Bal Thackeray. Further, in dismissing the application for a review petition, the Court was emphatic that the decision did not allow for an appeal to votes on the basis of religion. The decision was thus a contradictory one, in which the Hindu Right was both condemned and condoned. It is, moreover, the contradictory nature of the inroads made by the Hindu Right that continues to make law and legal discourse an important site of contestation in the struggle for Indian secularism. Despite the mounting pressure and influence of the Hindu Right, the Court retains an important critical distance, and as such, can continue to be an important site of struggle against the enemies of democratic secularism.

At the heart of the Hindu Right's approach to secularism is a policy of assimilation. It is a policy that aims at denying, and ultimately, obliterating cultural and religious minorities. It is a policy that is most specifically directed at the Muslim minority, but that also includes other religious minorities that pose any threat to, or are in any way different from, the dominant Hindu norm. The effort to defend secularism from the onslaught of the Hindu Right will thus require a direct confrontation over the issue of minority rights. Our suggestions for revitalizing the principle of secularism have attempted to engage with precisely this issue. Our suggestions regarding each of the three principles of secularism—equality, freedom of religion and toleration—

share common features, with the emphasis on group rights being the chief among them. Within this vision of secularism, cultural minorities must be free to pursue their own beliefs, and the state must be willing to accommodate their group difference. The substantive approach to equality, to freedom of religion and to toleration, each emphasizes this accommodation of difference. In stark contrast to the approach of the Hindu Right, and other right wing discourses that emphasize equal treatment and assimilation of difference, the approach that we are outlining is one that insists on the democratic validity and necessity of accommodating difference. The damage inflicted by the *Hindutva* decisions can only be mended through a substantive notion of equality, a strategic deployment of a politically-based concept of toleration that sits on the citadel of respect, and an expanded understanding of the meaning of freedom of religion.

We have argued that a revisioning of secularism in legal discourse requires, at the minimum, a reclaiming of these three primary attributes of secularism. Equality must be wrestled away from the formalism of the Hindu Right, and reimbued with its spirit of egalitarianism that can recognize and accommodate cultural minorities and disadvantaged groups. The courts should direct greater attention to unmasking the unstated norms of the majority that lurk in the shadows of formal equality, and shift their inquiries to a more substantive model of equality. Equality cannot remain the exclusive preserve of the majority community, and it can only be democratized through an analysis that is attentive to issues of historic and systemic disadvantage. Freedom of religion must similarly be wrestled away from the narrow individualism of the Hindu Right, and reinfused with its collectivist dimensions. Again, the freedom to practise one's religion cannot be defined exclusively from the point of view of the dominant community. Rather, the courts must attempt to untie the right of freedom of religion from the unstated norms of the majority and recognize the importance of this right to religious minorities in India. This is all the more important given that the right to freedom of religion is the Achilles' heel of the Right's discourse, in so far as it is one of the attributes of secularism that has remained relatively free from their hegemonizing mission.

Finally, we need to work our way through the complex understanding of toleration that gives Indian secularism its distinct character. We have argued against those who have set up toleration in antagonism with secularism, and who argue for a vision of toleration that accepts the religious nature of Indian society and searches for the authentic roots of each religious tradition which must then be respected. Such archaeological expeditions are misguided at best and unworkable at worst as they assume that there is a purity of culture that can be excavated and restored in all its pristine glory. This analysis ignores the fact that India is a country that itself was forged on the anvil of colonialism, and the traditions of the subcontinent have been re-configured and re-shaped through invasions, wars and colonial rule. There is no possibility of returning to authenticity, as all religious traditions have been hybridized through the history of global expansion and imperialism. Instead, we have argued for a political conception of toleration— one that is not ensnared in religious and majoritarian traps, but rather can recognize and accommodate differences within minority communities, provided these communities demon- strate democratic accountability and respect to their own members.

These three principles need to be taken up by the courts, in a manner that goes beyond the general articulation of the principle of equal respect for all religions. The general principle of secularism needs to be given much more specific content, and to have its underlying philosophical basis fully explored. It is only in so doing that the courts can play their important role in unmasking the deeply unsecular and undemocratic nature of the claims of the Hindu Right. It is only in so doing that we can more clearly demarcate the kinds of state action that are mandated by the protection of secularism—and it is only in so doing that we can hope to promote a truly democratic secularism in India.

The struggle to safeguard our vision of secularism cannot be limited to legal discourse alone. Law is an important site of struggle given its authoritative value. Yet it cannot fend off the incursions by the tentacles of right wing ideology in isolation. There is a need to adopt a multi-faceted attack on the Hindu Right's version of secularism. In so doing, it is important that the Hindu Right is not approached as omnipotent or homogeneous. Challenging their footholds of intolerance and hatred will require revealing the fragmentation, contradictions and conflicts within their own hierarchy, and exploiting the dissension and dissonance present within their ranks.

At the end of the day, conceptions of secularism will shift with changing political and historical contexts. There needs to be constant vigilance over the ways in which secularism is deployed. Secularism will remain a contested terrain whose image and features can be altered and re-moulded by those into whose hands it falls, or who seize it as their own. For the moment, secularism is hostage to the agenda of the Hindu Right. In this book we have tried to suggest ways in which to release it from its current religious bondage through a reconfiguration that will reclaim secularism as a unifying rather than divisive, fragmenting concept. It is but one effort to bring down the reign of Hindutva and the false godheads of Hinduism.

Appendix

DR RAMESH YESHWANT PRABHOO (APPELLANT) v. SHRI PRABHAKAR KASHINATH KUNTE & OTHERS (RESPONDENTS)

Date of Judgment : 11.12.95
Judgment by Justice Verma,
Bench: Justice Verma, Justice Singh, Justice Venkataswami

CITATIONS:
AIR 1996 SC 1113; 1996 (1) SCC 130

Civil Appeal No. 2836 with Civil Appeal No. 2835 of 1989, *Bal Thackeray v. Shri Prabhakar Kashinath Kunte & Others*

Justice J. S. VERMA:

1. Both these appeals are under Section 116A of the Representation of the People Act, 1951 (hereinafter referred to as 'the Act/R.P. Act') against the judgment dated 7th April, 1989 of the Bombay High Court in Election petition No. 1 of 1988 by which the election of Dr Ramesh

Yeshwant Prabhoo, the returned candidate from Vile Parle Constituency to the Maharashtra State Legislative Assembly, held on 13th December, 1987, has been declared to be void on the ground under Section 100(1)(b) of the Act. The appellant has been found guilty of the corrupt practices prescribed by sub-Sections (3) and (3A) of Section 123 of the Act at the election, in that he and his agent Bal Thackeray with his consent appealed for votes on the ground of the returned candidate's religion and that they promoted or tended to promote feelings of enmity and hatred between different classes of the citizens of India on the grounds of religion and community. Consequently, Bal Thackeray, after a notice issued under Section 99 of the Act to him, has also been named for commission of these corrupt practices. Civil Appeal No. 2836 of 1989 is by the returned candidate Dr Ramesh Yeshwant Prabhoo and Civil Appeal No. 2835 of 1989 is by Bal Thackeray against that judgment.

2. The said election was held on 13th December, 1987 and the result was declared on 14th December, 1987, at which Dr Ramesh Yeshwant Prabhoo was declared to be duly elected. The charge of these corrupt practices is based on three public speeches delivered by Bal Thackeray: on 29.11.1987 at Parle (opposite Shiv Sena Shaka No. 84), on 9.12.1987 at Khar-Danda near Shankar Temple, and on 10.12.1987 at Jaltaran Maidan, Vile Parle (East). The public speech given on 9.12.1987 has been held to amount to the corrupt practice under sub-section (3) of Section 123, while public speeches delivered on 29.11.1987 and 10.12.1987 have been held to be corrupt practices under sub-sections (3) and (3A) of Section 123 of the Act. The relevant pleading relating to these corrupt practices is contained in paras 6 and 8 of the election petition. Sub-paras (a) to (d) of para 6 relate to first speech, sub-para (e) of para 6 relates to second speech and sub-para (f) of para 6 relates to third speech. Para 8 of the election petition then says that returned candidate indulged in the corrupt practices provided by sub-sections (3) and (3A) of Section 123 of the Act and, therefore, his election is void.

3. After the election petitioner closed his evidence, the returned candidate Dr Prabhoo examined only himself in rebuttal. After close of the evidence of the parties and hearing arguments of both sides, the High Court ordered issue of notice under Section 99 of the Act to

Bal Thackeray who filed an affidavit in reply to the notice. The election petitioner and his three witnesses were recalled for cross-examination by counsel for the notice, Bal Thackeray. The notice did not examine himself or any other witness in rebuttal. The decision of the High Court is based on this material.

4. Dr Prabhoo was set up as candidate of the Shiv Sena which was then not a recognised political party for purposes of the Legislative Assembly elections and, therefore, Dr Prabhoo's candidature was shown as 'Shiv Sena -Independent'. Bal Thackeray is the top leader of Shiv Sena and he participated in the election campaign of Dr Prabhoo as the main speaker in his capacity as the leader of Shiv Sena. The status of Bal Thackeray as the top leader of Shiv Sena has never been disputed. The gist of election petitioner's case which has been found proved by the High Court is that the three public speeches of Bal Thackeray in the election campaign of Dr Prabhoo were all in very intemperate language and incendiary in nature which were appeals to the voters to vote for Dr Prabhoo because of his religion, i.e., he being a Hindu, and the speeches also promoted or tended to promote enmity and hatred between different classes of the citizens of India on the ground of religion. The High Court has held this charge of the alleged corrupt practices proved against the returned candidate Dr Prabhoo and Bal Thackeray. Accordingly, the election of the returned candidate has been declared to be void on the ground contained in Section 100(1) (b) of the Act, and Bal Thackeray has been named in accordance with Section 99 of the Act. Hence these appeals by them.

5. The averments in para 6 of the election petition alleging the commission of corrupt practices within the meaning of Section 123 of the Act are in sub-paras (a) to (f) which are as under:

> (a) The petitioner states that respondent No. 1, during his election campaign, indulged in corrupt practices by appealing himself, or by his election agents, or by his supporters with his consent to vote him and refrain from voting other candidates on the grounds of religion. The whole tenor of election propaganda of the respondent No. 1 was that he is a candidate of Hindus and Hindus

should vote him alone. The details of this appeal are given in the later part of this petition.

(b) The respondent No. 1, his election agents and his supporters with the consent of the candidate respondent No. 1 also indulged in corrupt practice by promoting and by attempting to promote feelings of enmity and hatred between different classes of citizens of India on grounds of religion, community and language. The examples of this corrupt practice are also listed in the later part of this petition.

(c) The campaign for the election of respondent No. 1 was headed by Shri Balasaheb Thackeray, the leader of the Shiv Sena, who had put up respondent No. 1 in this election. Shri Thackeray addressed several meetings and also issued press statements during the course of the election in question. Out of these meetings Shri Thackeray spoke on 29.11.1987 at a meeting held at Shiv Sena Shaka no. 84 at Vile Parle, which took place from 9 p.m. to 12 midnight. In this meeting Shri Balasaheb Thackeray, Suryakant Mahadik, Pramod Navalkar, Ramesh Mehta, Madhukar Sarpotdar and the candidate respondent No. 1 Dr Ramesh Prabhoo himself were also present. Shri Thackeray uttered the following words during this meeting. The words are quoted in Marathi and they are followed by the English translation.

> Translation: 'We are fighting this election for the protection of Hinduism. Therefore, we do not care for the votes of the Muslims. This country belongs to Hindus and will remain so.'

Since the petitioner was all throughout [sic] in the constituency for his election campaign, he came to know about the said meeting having been held and attended by Shri Bal Thackeray. Subsequently, he also came to know about the speeches made in the meeting from his friends and active workers of the Party. The petitioner has reliably learnt that the police reporters also attended the meeting and they have taken down the report of the speeches made. The petitioner craves leave to call for the record of the speeches from the Police Department and to prove the point by examining the police reporters who have taken down the speeches. The petitioner craves leave to rely upon the said police report in the custody of the Police. A report regarding the said meeting and the speeches appeared in the newspaper *Mumbai Sakal* (a Marathi daily) dated 1.12.1987 with the photographs under the title *Hindu Dev-devtavareel Teeka Sahan Karnar Nahi—Thackeray* (We will not tolerate the criticism of Hindu gods and goddesses—Thackeray). From the said photograph it is clear that respondent No. 1 was also present in the said meeting. Thus all the utterances regarding the speeches made by Bal Thackeray to appeal to voters in the name of Hindu religion are with the consent and connivance of the first respondent. The same meeting was also reported in *Sanj Tarun Bharat* (an evening daily) dated 30.11.87 with the photograph of Shri Thackeray, respondent No. 1 and others on the dias. The said photograph further shows that a banner was put up on the dias which reads as under:

Garva Say Kaho (OM) Ham Hindu Hai

The said meeting was also reported in *Sandhyakal*, another Marathi daily, on 1.12.87. Hereto annexed and marked Exhibit 'B' and 'B-1' is the original report appearing in *Sanj Tarun Bharat* with English translation and hereto annexed and marked Exhibit 'C' and 'C-1' is the said report appearing in *Sandhyakal* with English translation.

(d) The petitioner says that a report regarding the said meeting also appeared in the *Urdu Times*, an Urdu daily published from Bombay in its issue dated 1.12.87. The petitioner does not know how to read and write Urdu. However, he got the said report translated. In the said *Urdu Times* the report appeared with the title *Shiv Sena ko Musalmano ke votoki zarurat nahin hai* (Shiv Sena did not need the votes of Muslims). A true English translation of the said news item is annexed hereto and marked Exhibit

'D' and 'D-1' with a Xerox copy of the report in Urdu.

(e) Again on 9.12.87 there was another election meeting which took place from 9 a.m. to about 12 midnight at Khar-Danda, near Shankar Temple. This meeting was addressed by Shri Bal Thackeray, respondent No. 1, Harish Chandra Dattaji Salvi (a Shiv Sena leader) and Shambhoo Maharaj, a religious leader from Gujarat. In the said meeting Shri Bal Thackeray, while addressing the audience, stated as under:

> Translation: 'Hinduism will triumph in this election and we must become hon'ble recipients of this victory to ward off the danger on Hinduism, elect Ramesh Prabhoo to join with Chhagan Bhujbal who is already there. You will find Hindu temples underneath if all the mosques are dug out. Anybody who stands against the Hindus should be showed or worshipped with shoes. A candidate by name Prabhoo should be led to victory in the name of religion.'

The petitioner says that the proceedings of the said meeting were recorded by the police. Newspaper reports regarding the meeting also appeared. The petitioner will crave leave to and rely upon the records of the police and also the press report giving the version of the said meeting appearing in various newspapers.

(f) The petitioner says that on 10.12.87, a meeting was held from 9 p.m. to about 12 midnight at Vile Parle (East) at Shahaji Raje Marg. This was addressed by Shri Bal Thackeray, Shambhoo Maharaj, Ramesh Mehta, Rishi Kapoor, Jitendra Madhukar Joshi and Ramesh Prabhoo, respondent No. 1. In this meeting Shri Thackeray uttered the following words while addressing the meeting:

> Translation: 'We have come with the ideology of Hinduism. Shiv Sena will implement this ideology. Though this country belongs to Hindus, Ram and Krishna are insulted. (They) valued the Muslim votes more than your votes; we do not want the Muslim

votes. A snake like Shahabuddin is sitting in the Janata Party, a man like Nihal Ahmed is also in the Janata Party. So the residents of Vile Parle should bury this party (Janata Party).'

The above utterances in these three meetings are the examples of promoting the feelings of enmity between different classes of citizens of India. The sole purpose in doing so and making the appeal was to canvas votes in favour of the first respondent on the ground of religion and make it appear to the voters that respondent No. 1 was the only person who could represent the Hindu community. The effect of the said speeches was to promote the feelings of enmity and hatred between Hindus and non-Hindus on the ground of religion, race, caste, community etc. As such the petitioner and most of the respondents from 1 to 13 are Hindus, having full faith in the Hindu religion. The main ground of objection on the way of canvassing for votes by respondent No. 1 and his supporters was to bring the element of religion into politics endangering the very foundation of the Constitution of India, viz. secularism. The petitioner honestly believes that it is one thing to follow one's own religion according to one's own conviction and another thing to appeal to the voters to vote in the name of the religion.

6. Reliance was placed by the election petitioner on certain news items wherein the public speeches were published and also on certain reports alleged to have been made by some police officers who reported the making of the speeches raising some controversy relating to sufficiency of pleadings and the use of material for proving the contents of the speeches in excess of the exact words pleaded in the election petition. Details of this controversy would be mentioned later while considering that point. However, it may be mentioned that the extent to which there is specific pleading and the returned candidate himself admitted the contents of the public speeches can safely be considered subject to the objection raised of the alleged legal infirmities

including want of a valid notice under Section 99 of the Act to the noticee, Bal Thackeray. More details of the evidence would be mentioned at the appropriate stage.

7. Broadly stated, the contentions of Shri Ram Jethmalani, learned counsel for the appellants in these appeals, are:

(1) Sub-sections (3) and (3A) of Section 123 of the Act are constitutionally invalid being violative of guarantee of free speech in Article 19(1)(a) of the Constitution;

(2) To save both these provisions from constitutional invalidity, they must be read as reasonable restrictions in the interest of public order to get the protection of Article 19(2) of the Constitution. In other words, unless the speech is prejudicial to the maintenance of public order, it cannot fall within the net of either sub-section (3) or sub-section (3A) of Section 123 of the Act;

(3) In sub-section (3) of Section 123, the emphasis is on the word 'his' preceding the word 'religion' and its significance must be understood in the light of the restricted scope of the provision indicated by the Union Law Minister during the Parliamentary debates to explain the object of introduction of the word 'his' in the provision. In other words, only a direct appeal for votes on the ground of 'his' religion subject to its tendency to prejudice the maintenance of public order is contended to be the limited scope of sub-section (3) of Section 123;

(4) A speech in which there be a reference to religion but no direct appeal for votes on the ground of his religion, does not come within the net of sub-section (3) of Section 123;

(5) The public speeches in question did not amount to appeal for votes on the ground of his religion and the substance and main thrust thereof was 'Hindutava' [sic] which means the Indian culture and not merely the Hindu religion;

(6) The public speeches criticized the anti-secular stance of the Congress Party in practising discrimination against Hindus and giving undue favour to the minorities which is not an appeal for votes on the ground of Hindu religion;

(7) On behalf of the noticee Bal Thackeray, it was further contended that there was no compliance of the requirements of Section 99 of the

Act, inasmuch as the notice contemplated by the provision was not given and the noticee was never informed of the precise charge against him. It was submitted that the notice given was not in conformity with the law and particulars required to be given by the court were never given, the High Court having merely asked the petitioner to indicate the particulars of the charge of the corrupt practice; and

(8) that the pleadings in the election petition are deficient being devoid of the material particulars and, therefore, the material brought in at the stage of evidence and relied on to prove the charge of corrupt practice has to be excluded from consideration. Learned counsel for the appellant also made the grievance that the High Court had decided the election petition mainly on the basis of the general impressions and vague assertions made by the election petitioner instead of confining the decision to the precise pleadings and the legally admissible evidence examined in the light of the true meaning and scope of sub-sections (3) and (3A) of Section 123 of the Act.

8. In reply, Shri Ashok Desai, learned counsel for the respondent, refuted these contentions. He submitted that the question of constitutional validity of the provisions is no longer *res integra* being concluded by the decision of the Constitution Bench in *Jamuna Prasad Mukhariya & Others v. Lachhi Ram & Others*, 1955 (1) SCR 608: AIR 1954 SC 686. Alternatively, he contended that the freedom of speech guaranteed in the Constitution does not extend to giving speeches of the kind given by Bal Thackeray and, at any rate, these provisions impose reasonable restrictions on the freedom of speech which are saved by Article 19(2) of the Constitution. Shri Desai also submitted that the substance and main thrust of the speech, not merely the form, has to be seen in its context to determine if it amounts to an appeal for votes on the ground of 'his' religion, and such appeal need not necessarily be only direct. Learned counsel submitted that each one of the speeches in question was highly incendiary containing appeal [sic] to vote for Dr Ramesh Prabhoo because he is a Hindu; and it also tended to promote enmity and hatred between Hindus and Muslims. According to him, each one of the speeches amounted to the corrupt practice both under sub-sections (3) and (3A) of Section 123 of the Act.

MEANING OF SUB-SECTIONS (3) AND (3A) OF SECTION 123 OF THE R.P. ACT

9. Sub-sections (3) and (3A) of Section 123 of the R.P. Act are as under:

123. Corrupt practices. The following shall be deemed to be corrupt practices for the purposes of this Act:

(3) The appeal by a candidate or his agent or by any other person with the consent of a candidate or his election agent to vote or refrain from voting for any person on the ground of his religion, race, caste, community, or language or the use of, or appeal to religious symbols or the use of, or appeal to, national symbols, such as the national flag or the national emblem, for the furtherance of the prospects of the election of that candidate or for prejudicially affecting the election of any candidate:

Provided that no symbol allotted under this Act to a candidate shall be deemed to be a religious symbol or a national symbol for the purposes of this clause.

(3A) The promotion of, or attempt to promote, feelings of enmity or hatred between different classes of the citizens of India on grounds of religion, race, caste, community, or language, by a candidate or his agent or any other person with the consent of a candidate or his election agent for the furtherance of the prospects of the election of that candidate or for prejudicially affecting the election of any candidate.

10. The submission of Shri Ram Jethmalani, learned counsel for the appellants is that the appeal to vote or refrain from voting for any person on the ground of 'his' religion, etc. for the furtherance of the prospects of the election of that candidate or for prejudicially affecting the election of any candidate, means a direct appeal to vote or refrain from voting on the ground of 'his' religion, etc.; and the appeal must

also be provocative in nature to adversely affect public order. The further element of adverse effect on public order, it is urged, is implicit in the provision to save it from constitutional invalidity, which argument is considered separately. Shri Jethmalani laid emphasis on the word 'his' which was inserted by Act 40 of 1961 w.e.f. 20.9.1961 when the existing sub-section (3) was substituted for the old sub-section (3). Shri Jethmalani contended that the object of insertion of the word 'his' in the newly substituted sub-section (3) was to restrict the meaning of the provision and confine it only to a direct appeal based on 'his' religion. Learned counsel placed strong reliance on the statement of the Law Minister during the debates in the Parliament to support this submission. In reply, Shri Ashok Desai, learned counsel for the respondent contended that the word 'his' no doubt has significance, but its use does not confine the meaning of sub-section (3) only to a direct appeal on the ground of 'his' religion, etc. and extends to an appeal of which the main thrust in the context is on the religion of the candidate. Shri Desai submitted that an unduly restricted meaning cannot be given to sub-section (3) since the object of the provision is to prohibit appeal for votes during the election on the ground of religion of the candidate.

11. There can be no doubt that the word 'his' used in sub- section (3) must have significance and it cannot be ignored or equated with the word 'any' to bring within the net of sub-section (3) any appeal in which there is any reference to religion. The religion forming the basis of the appeal to vote or refrain from voting for any person, must be of that candidate for whom the appeal to vote or refrain from voting is made. This is clear from the plain language of sub-section (3) and this is the only manner in which the word 'his' used therein can be construed. The expressions 'the appeal...to vote or refrain from voting for any person on the ground of his religion,...for the furtherance of the prospects of the election of that candidate or for prejudicially affecting the election of any candidate' lead clearly to this conclusion. When the appeal is to vote on the ground of 'his' religion for the furtherance of the prospects of the election of that candidate, that appeal is made on the basis of the religion of the candidate for whom votes are solicited. On the other hand when the appeal is to refrain from voting for any person on the ground of 'his' religion for

prejudicially affecting the election of any candidate, that appeal is based on the religion of the candidate whose election is sought to be prejudicially affected. It is thus clear that for soliciting votes for a candidate, the appeal prohibited is that which is made on the ground of religion of the candidate for whom the votes are sought; and when the appeal is to refrain from voting for any candidate, the prohibition is against an appeal on the ground of the religion of that other candidate. The first is a positive appeal and the second a negative appeal. There is no ambiguity in sub-section (3) and it clearly indicates the particular religion on the basis of which an appeal to vote or refrain from voting for any person is prohibited under sub-section (3).

12. The argument that such an appeal must be a direct appeal, such as 'Vote for A because he is a Hindu' or 'Do not vote for B because he is a Christian', and that no other appeal leading to that conclusion is forbidden, does not appeal to reason. What is forbidden by sub-section (3) is an appeal of this kind and, therefore, any appeal which amounts to or leads to this inference must necessarily come within the prohibition in sub-section (3). Whether a particular appeal is of this kind, is a question of fact in each case. Where the words used in the appeal are clear and unambiguous amounting to a direct appeal, the exercise of construing the speech is not needed. However, where a reasonable construction of the appeal leads to that conclusion, the result must be the same. The substance of the speech and the manner in which it is meant to be understood by the audience determines its nature, and not the camouflage by an artistic use of the language. For understanding the meaning and effect of the speech, the context has to be found in the speech itself and not outside it with reference to any other background unless the speech itself imports any earlier fact in the context of that speech. The speech has also not to be construed in the abstract or in the manner in which it would be construed after an academic debate. Care must be taken to remember that the public speeches during election campaign ordinarily are addressed to an audience comprised of common men and, therefore, the manner in which it would be understood by such an audience has to be kept in view.

13. We are unable to accept the submission of Shri Jethmalani that a further element of prejudicial effect on public order, is implicit in sub-section (3). We do not find anything in the language of the

provision to read this further element into it. Sub-section (3) in substance forbids appeal for votes for any candidate on the ground of 'his' religion and appeal to refrain from voting for any other candidate on the ground of the religion of that other candidate. Obviously the purpose of enacting the provision is to ensure that no candidate at an election gets votes only because of his religion and no candidate is denied any votes on the ground of his religion. This is in keeping with the secular character of the Indian polity and rejection of the scheme of separate electorates based on religion in our constitutional scheme. An appeal of the kind forbidden by sub-section (3) based on the religion of a candidate, need not necessarily be prejudicial to public order and, therefore, the further element of likelihood of prejudice to public order is unnecessary, on account of which it is not implicit in the provision. This, according to us, is the meaning and the correct construction of sub-section (3). The question of constitutional validity of the provision on this meaning is considered later.

14. Reference may now be made to the Parliamentary debates in which the reason ascribed by the Law Minister Shri A.K. Sen for adding the word 'his' in sub-section (3) and its purpose was stated, thus—

'Shri A. K. Sen: I added the word 'his' in the Select Committee in order to make quite clear as to what was the mischief which was sought to be prevented under this provision.'

'Shri A. K. Sen: The apprehension was expressed if one's right was going to be curbed by this section. If such a right was going to be curbed by the section, I would have been against such an amendment, because after all, it is the right of a person to propagate his own language, his own particular culture and various other matters. But that does not mean vilifying another language or creating enmity between communities.'

'Shri A. K. Sen: I am pained to hear Shri Hynniewta giving expression to an apprehension, which to me seems entirely baseless. That apprehension is to the effect that clause 23 will deprive him of his right to propagate his language or preserve his language, which cannot be taken away from him as he himself has quoted the relevant article of the Constitution. If that right is taken away by the Bill, it will be struck down as contravening article 19 and the section will not be given effect to by any court. Fortunately, this country is still governed by the rule of law and the courts of law have the last say in these matters.'

'Shri A. K. Sen: That is a different matter. With due respect to the hon. Member, he has not really appreciated the rationale of the Supreme Court's decision. With regard to election matters, Parliament is free to enact such legislation as it thinks best and Chapter III does not come in. That is the decision of the Supreme Court. But in the guise of framing an electoral law, no fundamental right of the citizen can be taken away. That is what I am saying. The right to preserve one's language cannot be taken away by an election law. That is as clear as daylight.'

'Shri A. K. Sen: You cannot make it an election issue if you say, 'Do not vote for him. He is a Bengali' or 'Do not vote for him. He is a Khasi'. I made it unequivocally clear that it is the purpose and design of this House and of the country to ensure that. No man shall appeal only because he speaks a particular language and should get voted for that reason; or no man shall appeal against a particular person to the electorate solely because that opponent of his speaks a particular language.'

'Shri A. K. Sen: They are not entitled to do so. But we are on a very narrow point, whether we shall extend the right to a person, to a voter, to say: vote for me because I speak Hindi, I speak Garhwali, or I speak Nepali or I speak Khasi; or in the alternative, do not vote for my opponent because he is a man who speaks this particular language, his own language. It is on that sole narrow point that the prohibition is sought to be made....But we are not here to discuss the aesthetics of language or the philosophy of language; nor are we here to debate the fundamental rights of a citizen to preserve his own language and culture. Fortunately, that is guaranteed to every man and woman in this country as it is not elsewhere....'

'Shri A. K. Sen: The problem is, are we going to allow a man to go to the electorate and ask for votes because he happens to speak a particular language or ask the electorate to refrain from voting for a particular person merely on the ground of his speaking a particular language or following a particular religion and so on? If not, we have to support this. The preservation of the minority's rights and so on is a different and a wider question.'

'Shri A.K. Sen:... But, if you say that Bengali language in this area is being suppressed or the schools are being closed as Shri Hynniewta was saying, because they bore a particular name, then, you are speaking not only to fight in an election but you are also really seeking to protect your fundamental rights, to preserve your own language and culture. That is a different matter.

But, if you say, 'I am a Bengali, you are all Bengalis, vote for me', or 'I am an Assamese and so vote for me because you are Assamese speaking men', I think, the entire House will deplore that as a hopeless form of election propaganda. And, no progressive party will run an election on that line. Similarly, on the ground of religion. In the olden days, what speeches we used to hear in Muslim League gatherings! They were purely appeals on the ground of religion. So, the issue is too narrow and not a wide issue in which the life and death of minorities are involved as Shri Hynniewta sought to make out. It is not at all in question...'

15. The clarification given in the speech of the Law Minister clearly shows that a speech for the protection of fundamental rights, preservation of own language, religion and culture, etc. are not forbidden by sub-section (3) of Section 123, and the limit is narrow to the extent indicated.

16. It cannot be doubted that a speech with a secular stance alleging discrimination against any particular religion and promising removal of the imbalance cannot be treated as an appeal on the ground of religion as its thrust is for promoting secularism. Instances given in the speech of discrimination against any religion causing the imbalance in the professed goal of secularism, the allegation being against any individual or any political party, cannot be called an appeal on the ground of religion forbidden by sub-section (3). In other words, mention of religion as such in an election speech is not forbidden by sub-section (3) so long as it does not amount to an appeal to vote for

a candidate on the ground of his religion or to refrain from voting for any other candidate on the ground of his religion. When it is said that politics and religion do not mix, it merely means that the religion of a candidate cannot be used for gaining political mileage by seeking votes on the ground of the candidate's religion or alienating the electorate against another candidate on the ground of the other candidate's religion. It also means that the state has no religion and the State practises the policy of neutrality in the matter of religion.

In *Dr M. Ismail Faruqui & Others etc. v. Union of India & Others etc.*, 1994 (6) SCC 360: (1994 AIR SCW 4897) (Ayodhya case), the Constitution Bench, after a detailed discussion, summarized the true concept of secularism under the Indian Constitution as under:

> 'It is clear from the constitutional scheme that it guarantees equality in the matter of religion to all individuals and groups irrespective of their faith emphasizing that there is no religion of the State itself. The Preamble of the Constitution read in particular with Articles 25 to 28 emphasizes this aspect and indicates that it is in this manner the concept of secularism embodied in the constitutional scheme as a creed adopted by the Indian people has to be understood while examining the constitutional validity of any legislation on the touchstone of the Constitution. The concept of secularism is one facet of the right to equality woven as the central golden thread in the fabric depicting the pattern of the scheme in our Constitution.' (at p. 403 of SCC): (at p. 4392 of AIR).

18. It cannot be doubted that an election speech made in conformity with the fundamental right to freedom of religion guaranteed under Articles 25 to 30 of the Constitution, cannot be treated as anti-secular to be prohibited by sub-section (3) of Section 123, unless it falls within the narrow net of the prohibition indicated earlier. It is obvious that a speech referring to religion during election campaign with a secular stance in conformity with the fundamental right to freedom of religion can be made without being hit by the prohibition contained in sub-section (3), if it does not contain an appeal to vote for any candidate because of his religion or to refrain from voting for any candidate

because of his religion. When it is said that politics and religion do not mix, it obviously does not mean that even such permissible political speeches are forbidden. This is the meaning and true scope of sub-section (3) of Section 123 of the Act.

19. We would now consider the meaning of sub-section (3A) of Section 123. This sub-section also was inserted along with the substituted sub-section (3) by Act 40 of 1961 w.e.f. 20.9.1961. The meaning of this sub-section is not much in controversy. Sub-section (3A) is similar to section 153-A of the Indian Penal Code. In sub-section (3A), the expression used is 'the promotion of, or attempt to promote, feelings of enmity or hatred' as against the expression 'Whoever...promotes or attempts to promote...disharmony or feelings of enmity, hatred or ill-will...' in Section 153-A, I.P.C. The expression 'feelings of enmity or hatred' is common in both the provisions but the additional words in Section 153-A, I.P.C. are 'disharmony...or ill-will'. The difference in the plain language of the two provisions indicates that mere promotion of disharmony or ill-will between different groups of people is an offence under Section 153-A, I.P.C. while under sub-section (3A) of Section 123 of the R.P. Act, it is only the promotion of or attempt to promote feelings of enmity or hatred, which are stronger words, that is forbidden in the election campaign.

20. The provision is made with the object of curbing the tendency to promote or attempt to promote communal, linguistic or any other factional enmity or hatred to prevent the divisive tendencies. The provision in the I.P.C. as well as in the R.P. Act for this purpose was made by amendment at the same time. The amendment in the R.P. Act followed amendments made in the Indian Penal Code to this effect in a bid to curb any tendency to resort to divisive means to achieve success at the polls on the ground of religion or narrow communal or linguistic affiliations. Any such attempt during the election is viewed with disfavour under the law and is made a corrupt practice under sub-section (3A) of Section 123.

21. Shri Jethmalani is right that in sub-section (3A), the element of prejudicial effect on public order is implicit. Such divisive tendencies promoting enmity or hatred between different classes of citizens of India tend to create public unrest and disturb public order. This is a

logical inference to draw on proof of the constituent parts of sub-section (3A). The meaning of sub-section (3A) is not seriously disputed between the parties and, therefore, it does not require any further discussion. However, whether the act complained of falls within the net of sub-section (3A) is a question of fact in each case to be decided on the basis of the evidence led to prove the alleged act.

22. The decision in *Ziyauddin Burhanuddin Bukhari v. Brijmohan Ramdass Mehta & Others*, 1975 (Suppl.) SCR 281: (AIR 1975 SC 1788) lends assurance to the correctness of the construction made by us of these provisions. The returned candidate Bukhari was the candidate of Muslim League while the defeated candidate Shauket Chagla was the Congress candidate at the election. Both were Muslims. The returned candidate Bukhari in his appeal to the voters said that Chagla was not true to his religion while he himself was a true Muslim. The clear implication of the appeal was that Chagla was not true to his religion whereas Bukhari was, and, therefore, the voters should prefer Bukhari. In short, the appeal for votes was made on the ground that Bukhari was a staunch believer of the Muslim religion as against Chagla who did [sic] not. It was this clear appeal based on the ground of the candidate's religion which was held to constitute the corrupt practices defined by sub-sections (3) and (3A) of Section 123 of the R.P. Act. For this purpose, the true ambit and scope of these provisions was considered and indicated as under:

> 'We propose to indicate, at this stage, what mischief the provisions were designed to most illuminating and certain way of correctly construing these statutory provisions. We cannot do so without adverting to the historical, political, and Constitutional background of our democratic set up, such provisions are necessary in your opinion, to sustain the spirit or climate in which the electoral machinery of this set up could work (para 10 of AIR).

> Our Constitution-makers certainly intended to set up a Secular Democratic Republic, the binding spirit of which is summed up by the objectives set forth in the preamble to the Constitution. No democratic political and social order, in which the conditions of freedom and their

progressive expansion for all make some regulation of all activities imperative, could endure without an agreement on the basic essentials which could unite and hold citizens together despite all the differences of religion, race, caste, community, culture, creed and language. Our political history made it particularly necessary that these differences, which can generate powerful emotions depriving people of their powers of rational thought and action, should not be permitted to be exploited lest the imperative conditions for the preservation of democratic freedoms are disturbed (para 11 of AIR).

It seems to us that Section 123, sub-secs. (2), (3) and (3A) were enacted so as to eliminate, from the electoral process, appeals to those divisive factors which arouse irrational passions that run counter to the basic tenets of our Constitution, and, indeed, of any civilised political and social order. Due respect for the religious beliefs and practices, race, creed, culture and language of other citizens is one of the basic postulates of our democratic system. Under the guise of protecting your own religion, culture or creed you cannot embark on personal attacks on those of others or whip up low hard instincts and animosities or irrational fears between groups to secure electoral victories. The line has to be drawn by the Courts, between what is permissible and what is prohibited, after taking into account the facts and circumstances of each case interpreted in the context in which the statements or acts complained of were made (para 12 of AIR).

We have to determine the effect of statements proved to have been made by a candidate, or, on his behalf and with his consent, during his election, upon the minds and feelings of the ordinary average voters of this country in every case of alleged corrupt practice of undue influence by making statements. We will, therefore, proceed to consider the particular facts of the case before us (para 15 of AIR).

...In other words, Bukhari, apart from making a direct attack on the alleged religious beliefs and practices of the Chagla family, clearly conveyed to the hearers that Chagla was an unfit person, on the ground of his mixed religious faith and practices, to represent Muslims. Bukhari had also called upon Muslims to unite against such a person if they wanted their religion to survive. The High Court had very rightly held that these statements contravened the provisions of Section 123 (3) of the Act (para 36 of AIR).

We do not think that any useful purpose is served by citing authorities, as the learned Counsel for the appellant tried to do, to interpret the facts of the case before us by comparing them to the very different facts of other cases. In all such cases, the line has no doubt to be drawn with care so as not to equate possible impersonal attacks on religious bigotry and intolerance with personal ones actuated by bigotry and intolerance (para 39 of AIR).

As already indicated by us, our democracy can only survive if those who aspire to become people's representatives and leaders understand the spirit of secular democracy. That spirit was characterised by Montesquieu long ago as one of 'virtue'. It implies, as the late Pandit Jawaharlal Nehru once said, 'self discipline'. For such a spirit to prevail, candidates at elections have to try to persuade electors by showing them the light of reason and not by inflaming their blind and disruptive passions. Heresy hunting propaganda or professedly religious grounds directed against a candidate at an election may be permitted in a theocratic state but not in a secular republic like ours. It is evident that, if such propaganda was permitted here, it would injure the interests of members of religious minority groups more than those of others. It is forbidden in this country in order to preserve the spirit of equality, fraternity, and amity between rivals even during elections. Indeed, such prohibitions are necessary in the interests of elementary public peace and order (para 40 of AIR).

According to his own professions, the appellant wanted votes for himself on the ground that he staunchly adhered to what he believed to be Muslim religion as contrasted with Chagla who did not. There is no doubt whatsoever in our minds that the High Court had rightly found the appellant guilty of the corrupt practices defined by the provisions of Section 123 (2), 123(3) and 123(3A) of the Act by making the various speeches closely examined by us also' (para 47 of AIR).

The meaning of sub-sections (3) and (3A) of Section 123 was understood and indicated in this decision, in the above manner.

CONSTITUTIONAL VALIDITY OF SUB-SECTIONS (3) AND (3A) OF SECTION 123

23. The next question now relates to the constitutional validity of these provisions on the meaning ascribed to them.

24. Sub-section (3A) of Section 123 is undoubtedly a provision made in the interests of public order because the promotion or attempt to promote feelings of enmity or hatred between different classes of the citizens of India on any of the grounds specified therein, apart from creating divisive tendency, would also be prejudicial to the maintenance of public order and may amount to incitement to commission of offences. The freedom of speech and expression guaranteed to all citizens under Article 19(1)(a), which is the basis of the constitutional challenge to this provision, is subject to clause (2) of Article 19 which permits the making of any law imposing reasonable restrictions on the exercise of this right in the interests of public order or incitement to an offence. For this reason, no further attempt was made to press the argument of challenge to the constitutional validity of sub-section (3A) on the construction we have made of that provision.

25. The question now is of the constitutional validity of sub-section (3) of Section 123. We have already rejected the argument that the element of prejudicial effect on public order is implicit also in sub-section (3) as it is in sub- section (3A). According to Shri Ram

Jethmalani, unless this element also is read into sub-section (3), it is violative of Article 19(1)(a) inasmuch as clause (2) of Article 19 does not save its validity under any of the other heads specified therein.

26. We have construed sub-section (3) of Section 123 as a restriction only to the extent that votes cannot be sought for a candidate on the ground of his religion, etc. and similarly there can be no appeal to refrain from voting for any person on the same ground. In other words, an appeal to vote for a candidate or not to vote for him on the ground of his religion, etc. is the restriction imposed by sub-section (3). This restriction is in the law enacted to provide for the conduct of elections, the qualifications and disqualifications for membership of the Houses, the corrupt practices and other offences at or in connection with such elections. The right to contest the election is given by the statute subject to the conditions prescribed therein. The restriction is limited only to the appeal for votes to a candidate during the election period and not to the freedom of speech and expression in general or the freedom to profess, practise and propagate religion unconnected with the election campaign.

27. It is true, as argued by Shri Jethmalani, that the freedom of speech and expression guaranteed to all citizens under Article 19(1)(a) is absolute subject to the reasonable restrictions imposed by any law saved by clause (2) of Article 19, under one of the heads specified therein. The heads specified in clause (2) of Article 19 are, therefore, several and they are intended to cover the entire area within which the absolute freedom to say anything which the speaker may like would not extend, in keeping with the standards of a civilized society, the corresponding rights in others in an orderly society, and the constitutional scheme.

28. The expression 'in the interests of' used in clause (2) of Article 19 indicates a wide amplitude of the permissible law which can be enacted to provide for reasonable restrictions on the exercise of this right under one of the heads specified therein, in conformity with the constitutional scheme. Two of the heads mentioned are decency or morality. Thus any law which imposes reasonable restrictions on the exercise of this right in the interests of decency or morality is also saved by clause (2) of Article 19. Shri Jethmalani contended that the words

'decency or morality' relate to sexual morality alone. In view of the expression 'in the interests of' and the context of election campaign for a free and fair poll, the right to contest the election being statutory and subject to the provisions of the statute, the words 'decency or morality' do not require a narrow or pedantic meaning to be given to these words. The dictionary meaning of 'decency' is 'correct and tasteful standards of behaviour as generally accepted; conformity with current standards of behaviour or propriety; avoidance of obscenity; and the requirements of correct behaviour' (*The Oxford Encyclopedic English Dictionary*); 'conformity to the prevailing standards of propriety, morality, modesty, etc.: and the quality of being decent' (*Collins English Dictionary*).

29. Thus, the ordinary dictionary meaning of 'decency' indicates that the action must be in conformity with the current standards of behaviour or propriety, etc. In a secular polity, the requirement of correct behaviour or propriety is that an appeal for votes should not be made on the ground of the candidate's religion which by itself is no index of the suitability of a candidate for membership of the House. In *Knuller (Publishing, Printing and Promotions) Ltd. & Others·v. Director of Public Prosecutions*, 1972(2) All ER 898, the meaning of 'indecency' was indicated as under:

...Indecency is not confined to sexual indecency; indeed it is difficult to find any limit short of saying that it includes anything which an ordinary decent man or woman would find to be shocking, disgusting and revolting...(at page 905)

30. Thus, seeking votes at an election on the ground of the candidate's religion in a secular State, is against the norms of decency and propriety of the society.

31. In our opinion, the saving in clause (2) of Article 19 permits the imposition of reasonable restrictions on the exercise of the right conferred by Article 19(1)(a) by making any law in the interests of decency or morality; and sub-section (3) of Section 123 of the R.P. Act, as construed by us, has the protection of clause (2) of Article 19 under the head 'decency' therein. This conclusion is reached by us even if it is assumed that the provision is not saved merely as a condition subject to which the statutory right of contesting an election is

available to the candidate. The fact that the scheme of separate electorates was rejected in framing the Constitution and secularism is the creed adopted in the constitutional scheme, are relevant considerations to treat this as a reasonable restriction on the freedom of speech and expression, for maintaining the standard of behaviour required in conformity with the decency and propriety of the societal norms. Viewed at in any manner, sub-section (3) of Section 123 cannot be held to be unconstitutional. This view is also in accord with the nature of right to contest an election, as understood in *Jamuna Prasad Mukhariya & Others v. Lachhi Ram & Others*, 1955 (1) SCR 608: (AIR 1954 SC 686).

32. The argument assailing the constitutional validity of subsections (3) and/or (3A) of Section 123 is rejected.

MEANING OF 'HINDUTVA' AND 'HINDUISM'

33. The next contention relates to the meaning of 'Hindutva' and 'Hinduism' and the effect of the use of these expressions in the election speeches.

34. We have already indicated the meaning of sub-section (3) of Section 123 of the R.P. Act and the limit of its operation. It may be said straightaway that any speech wherein these expressions are used, irrespective of their meaning, cannot by itself fall within the ambit of sub-section (3) of Section 123, unless the speech can be construed as an appeal to vote for a candidate on the ground that he is a Hindu or to refrain from voting for a candidate on the ground of his religion, i.e., he not being a Hindu. We have also indicated that mere reference to any religion in an election speech does not bring it within the net of sub-section (3) and/or sub-section (3A) of Section 123, since reference can be made to any religion in the context of secularism or to criticize any political party for practising discrimination against any religious group or generally for preservation of the Indian culture. In short, mere use of the word 'Hindutva' or 'Hinduism' or mention of any other religion in an election speech does not bring it within the net of sub-section (3) and/or sub-section (3A) of Section 123, unless the further elements indicated are also present in that speech. It is also necessary to see the meaning and purport of the speech and the manner

in which it was likely to be understood by the audience to which the speech was addressed. These words are not to be construed in the abstract, when used in an election speech.

35. Both sides referred copiously to the meaning of the word 'Hindutva' and 'Hinduism' with reference to several writings. Shri Jethmalani referred to them for the purpose of indicating the several meanings of these words and to emphasise that the word 'Hindutva' relates to Indian culture based on the geographical division known as Hindustan, i.e., India. On the other hand, Shri Ashok Desai emphasised that the term 'Hindutva' used in election speeches is an emphasis on Hindu religion bearing no relation to the fact that India is also known as Hindustan, and the term can relate to Indian culture.

36. The Constitution Bench in *Sastri Yagnapurushadji and Others v. Muldas Bhudardas Vaishya and Another*, 1966 (3) SCR 242 held thus:

> 'Who are Hindus and what are the broad features of Hindu religion, that must be the first part of our enquiry in dealing with the present controversy between the parties. The historical and etymological genesis of the word 'Hindu' has given rise to a controversy amongst Indologists; but the view generally accepted by scholars appears to be that the word 'Hindu' is derived from the river Sindhu otherwise known as Indus which flows from the Punjab. 'That part of the great Aryan race', says Monier Williams, 'which immigrated from Central Asia, through the mountain passes into India, settled first in the districts near the river Sindhu (now called the Indus). The Persians pronounced this word Hindu and named their Aryan brethren Hindus. The Greeks, who probably gained their first ideas of India from the Persians, dropped the hard aspirate, and called the Hindus 'Indoi' (*Hinduism* by Monier Williams, p. 1).
>
> *The Encyclopaedia of Religion and Ethics*, Vol. VI, has described 'Hinduism' as the title applied to that form of religion which prevails among the vast majority of the present population of the Indian Empire (p. 686). As Dr Radhakrishnan has observed; 'The Hindu civilization

is so-called, since its original founders or earliest followers occupied the territory drained by the Sindhu (the Indus) river system corresponding to the North West Frontier Province and the Punjab. This is recorded in the Rig Veda, the oldest of the Vedas, the Hindu scriptures which give their name to this period of Indian history. The people on the Indian side of the Sindhu were called Hindu by the Persian and the later western invaders' (*The Hindu View of Life* by Dr Radhakrishnan, p. 12). That is the genesis of the word 'Hindu'.

When we think of the Hindu religion, we find it difficult, if not impossible, to define Hindu religion or even adequately describe it. Unlike other religions in the world, the Hindu religion does not claim any one prophet; it does not worship any one God; it does not subscribe to any one dogma; it does not believe in any one philosophical concept; it does not follow any one set of religious rites or performances; in fact, it does not appear to satisfy the narrow traditional features of any religion or creed. It may broadly be described as a way of life and nothing more.

...The term 'Hindu', according to Dr Radhakrishnan, had originally a territorial and not a credal significance. It implied residence in a well-defined geographical area. Aboriginal tribes, savage and half-civilized people, the cultured Dravidians and the Vedic Aryans' were all Hindus as they were the sons of the same mother. The Hindu thinkers reckoned with the striking fact that the men and women dwelling in India belonged to different communities, worshipped different gods, and practised different rites (*Kurma Purana*) (ibid p. 12).

Monier Williams has observed that 'it must be borne in mind that Hinduism is far more than a mere form of theism resting on Brahmanism. It presents for our investigation a complex congeries of creeds and doctrines which in its gradual accumulation may be compared to the gathering together of the mighty volume of the Ganges, swollen by a continual influx of tributary rivers and rivulets, spreading itself over an ever increasing area of country and finally resolving itself into an intricate delta of tortuous steams and jungly marshes... The Hindu religion is a reflection of the composite character of the Hindus, who are not one people but many. It is based on the idea of universal receptivity. It has ever aimed at accommodating itself to circumstances, and has carried on the process of adaptation through more than three thousand years. It has first borne with and then, so to speak, swallowed, digested, and assimilated something from all creeds'. (*Religious Thought & Life in India* by Monier Williams, p. 57).

We have already indicated that the usual tests which can be applied in relation to any recognised religion or religious creed in the world turn out to be inadequate in dealing with the problem of Hindu religion. Normally, any recognised religion or religious creed subscribes to a body of set philosophic concepts and theological beliefs. Does this test apply to the Hindu religion? In answering this question, we would base ourselves mainly on the exposition of the problem by Dr Radhakrishnan in his work on Indian philosophy. (*Indian Philosophy* by Dr Radhakrishnan, vol. I, pp 22–3). Unlike other countries, India can claim that philosophy in ancient India was not an auxiliary to any other science or art, but always held a prominent position of independence... 'In all the fleeting centuries of history', says Dr Radhakrishnan, 'in all the vicissitudes through which India has passed, a certain marked identity is visible. It has held fast to certain psychological traits which constitute its special heritage, and they will be the characteristic marks of the Indian people so long as they are privileged to have a separate existence'. The history of Indian thought emphatically brings out the fact that the development of Hindu religion has always been inspired by an endless quest of the mind for truth based on the consciousness that truth has many facets. Truth is one, but wise men describe it differently. (...)

The Indian mind has, consistently through the ages, been exercised over the problem of the nature of godhead, the problem that faces the spirit at the end of life, and the inter-relation between the individual and the universal soul. 'If we can abstract from the variety of opinion', says Dr Radhakrishnan, 'and observe the general spirit of Indian thought, we shall find that it has a disposition to interpret life and nature in the way of monistic idealism, though this tendency is so plastic, living and manifold that it takes many forms and expresses itself in even mutually hostile teachings'. (...)

...Naturally enough, it was realised by Hindu religion from the very beginning of its career that truth was many-sided and different views contained different aspects of truth which no one could fully express. This knowledge inevitably bred a spirit of tolerance and willingness to understand and appreciate the opponent's point of view. That is how 'the several views set forth in India in regard to the vital philosophical concepts are considered to be the branches of the self-same tree. The short cuts and blind alleys are somehow reconciled with the main road of advance to the truth.' (...) When we consider this broad sweep of the Hindu philosophical concepts, it would be realised that under Hindu philosophy, there is no scope for ex-communicating any notion or principle as heretical and rejecting it as such.

The development of Hindu religion and philosophy shows that from time to time saints and religious reformers attempted to remove from the Hindu thought and practices elements of corruption and superstition and that led to the formation of different sects. Buddha started Buddhism; Mahavir founded Jainism; Basava became the founder of Lingayat religion, Dnyaneshwar and Tukaram initiated the Varakari Cult; Guru Nanak inspired Sikhism; Dayananda founded Arya Samaj, and Chaitanya began Bhakti cult; and as a result of the teachings of Ramakrishna and Vivekananda, Hindu religion flowered into its most attractive, progressive and dynamic form. If we study the teachings of these saints and religious reformers, we would notice an amount of divergence in their respective views; but underneath that divergence, there is a kind of subtle indescribable unity which keeps them within the sweep of the broad and progressive Hindu religion.

...It is somewhat remarkable that this broad sweep of Hindu religion has been eloquently described by Toynbee. Says Toynbee: 'When we pass from the plane of social practice to the plane of intellectual outlook, Hinduism too comes out well by comparison with the religions and ideologies of the South-West Asian group. In contrast to these, Hinduism has the same outlook as the pre-Christian and pre-Muslim religions and philosophies of the Western half of the old world. Like them, Hinduism takes it for granted that there is more than one valid approach to truth and to salvation and that these different approaches are not only compatible with each other, but are complementary' (*The Present-Day Experiment in Western Civilisation* by Toynbee, pp 48–9).

The Constitution-makers were fully conscious of this broad and comprehensive character of Hindu religion; and so, while guaranteeing the fundamental right to freedom of religion, Explanation II to Art. 25 has made it clear that in sub-clause (b) of clause (2), the reference to Hindus shall be construed as including a reference to persons professing the Sikh, Jaina or Buddhist religion, and the reference to Hindu religious institutions shall be construed accordingly.' (from pp 259–66) (at pp 1128–31 of AIR)

37. In a later Constitution Bench decision in *Commr. Of Wealth Tax, Madras & Others v. Late R. Sridharan by L. Rs.*, (1976) Supp.

SCR 478, the meaning of the term 'Hinduism' as commonly understood is stated thus;

'...It is a matter of common knowledge, that Hinduism
embraces within self so many diverse forms of beliefs,
faiths, practices and worship that it is difficult to define
the term 'Hindu' with precision'.

The historical and etymological genesis of the word
'Hindu' has been succinctly explained by Chief Justice
Gajendragadkar in *Shastri Yagnapurushdasji & Others v.
Muldas Bhundardas Vaishya & Anr.* (AIR 1966 SC 1119).

In Unabridged Edition of Webster's *Third New International Dictionary of the English Language*, the term 'Hinduism' has been defined as meaning 'a complex body of
social, cultural and religious beliefs and practices evolved
in and largely confined to the Indian subcontinent and
marked by a caste system, an outlook tending to view all
forms and theories as aspects of one eternal being and
truth, a moksha, and the practice of the way of works, the
way of knowledge, or the way of devotion as the means
of release from the bond of rebirths; the way of life and
form of thought of a Hindu'.

In *Encyclopaedia Britannica* (15th Edition), the term
'Hinduism' has been defined as meaning 'the civilization
of Hindus' (originally, the inhabitants of the land of the
Indus River). It properly denotes the Indian civilization of
approximately the last 2000 years, which gradually evolved
from Vedism, the religion of the ancient Indo-European
who settled in India in the last centuries of the 2nd
millennium BC. Because it integrates a large variety of
heterogeneous elements, Hinduism constitutes a very
complex but largely continuous whole, and since it covers
the whole of life, it has religious, social, economic, literary,
and artistic aspects. As a religion, Hinduism is an utterly
diverse conglomerate of doctrines, cults, and way of life...
In principle, Hinduism incorporates all forms of belief and
worship without necessitating the selection or elimination

of any. The Hindu is inclined to revere the divine in every manifestation, whatever it may be, and is doctrinally tolerant, leaving others—including both Hindus and non-Hindus—whatever creed and worship practices suit them best. A Hindu may embrace a non-Hindu religion without ceasing to be a Hindu, and since the Hindu is disposed to think synthetically and to regard other forms of worship, strange gods, and divergent doctrines as inadequate rather than wrong or objectionable, he tends to believe that the highest divine powers complement each other for the well-being of the world and mankind. Few religious ideas are considered to be finally irreconcilable. The core of religion does not even depend on the existence or non-existence of God or on whether there is one god or many. Since religious truth is said to transcend all verbal definition, it is not conceived in dogmatic terms. Hinduism is then both a civilization and a conglomerate of religions, with neither a beginning, a founder, nor a central authority, hierarchy, or organization. Every attempt at a specific definition of Hinduism has proved unsatisfactory in one way or another, the more so because the finest Indian scholars of Hinduism including Hindus themselves, have emphasized different aspects of the whole'.

In his celebrated treatise *Gitarahasaya*, B. G. Tilak has given the following broad description of the Hindu religion:

'Acceptance of the Vedas with reverence; recognition of the fact that the means or ways of salvation are diverse; and realisation of the truth that the number of gods to be worshipped is large, that indeed is the distinguishing feature of Hindu religion'.

In *Bhagwan Koer v. J. C. Bose & Others*, (1904 ILR 31 Cal. 11), it was held that Hindu religion is marvellously catholic [sic] and elastic. Its theology is marked by eclecticism and tolerance and almost unlimited freedom of private worship...

This being the scope and nature of the religion, it is not strange that it holds within its fold men of divergent views and traditions which have very little in common except a vague faith in what may be called the fundamentals of the Hindu religion.' (at pages 481–2)

38. These Constitution Bench decisions, after a detailed discussion, indicate that no precise meaning can be ascribed to the terms 'Hindu', 'Hindutva' and 'Hinduism'; and no meaning in the abstract can confine it to the narrow limits of religion alone, excluding the content of Indian culture and heritage. It is also indicated that the term 'Hindutva' is related more to the way of life of the people in the subcontinent. It is difficult to appreciate how in the face of these decisions the term 'Hindutva' or 'Hinduism' per se, in the abstract, can be assumed to mean and be equated with narrow fundamentalist Hindu religious bigotry, or be construed to fall within the prohibition in sub-sections (3) and/or (3A) of Section 123 of the R.P. Act.

39. Justice Bharucha in *Dr M. Ismail Faruqui & Others v. Union of India & Others*, 1994 (6) SCC 360: (1994 AIR SCW 4897), (Ayodhya case), in the separate opinion for himself and Justice Ahmadi (as he then was), observed as under:

...Hinduism is a tolerant faith. It is that tolerance that has enabled Islam, Christianity, Zoroastrianism, Judaism, Buddhism, Jainism and Sikhism to find shelter and support upon this land... (at page 442) (of SCC): (at p. 4971, para 159 of AIR)

40. Ordinarily, Hindutva is understood as a way of life or a state of mind and it is not to be equated with, or understood as religious Hindu fundamentalism. In *Indian Muslims: The Need For A Positive Outlook* by Maulana Wahiduddin Khan, (1994), it is said:

The strategy worked out to solve the minorities problem was, although differently worded, that of Hindutva or Indianisation. This strategy, briefly stated, aims at developing a uniform culture by obliterating the differences between all the cultures coexisting in the country. This was felt to be the way to communal harmony and national unity. It was thought that this would put an end once and for all to the minorities problem. (at page 19)

The above opinion indicates that the word 'Hindutva' is used and understood as a synonym of 'Indianisation', i.e., development of uniform culture by obliterating the differences between all the cultures co-existing in the country.

41. In *Kultar Singh v. Mukhtiar Singh*, 1964 (7) SCR 790: (AIR 196 SSC 141), the Constitution Bench construed the meaning of sub-section (3) of Section 123 prior to its amendment. The question there was whether a poster contained an appeal to voters to vote for the candidate on the ground of his religion; and the meaning of the word 'Panth' in the poster was significant for the purpose. It was held as under:

It is true that a corrupt practice under s. 123(3) can be committed by a candidate by appealing to the voters to vote for him on the ground of his religion even though his rival candidate may belong to the same religion. If, for instance, a Sikh candidate were to appeal to the voters to vote for him, because he was a Sikh in name, was not true to the religious tenets of Sikhism or was a heretic and as such, outside the pale of the Sikh religion, that would amount to a corrupt practice under s. 123(3), and so, we cannot uphold the contention that s. 123(3) is inapplicable because both the appellant and the respondent are Sikhs...

The corrupt practice as prescribed by s. 123(3) undoubtedly constitutes a very healthy and salutary provision which is intended to serve the cause of secular democracy in this country. In order that the democratic process should thrive and succeed, it is of utmost importance that our elections to Parliament and the different legislative bodies must be free from the unhealthy influence of appeals to religion, race, caste, community, or language. If these considerations are allowed any sway in election campaigns, they would vitiate the secular atmosphere of democratic life, and so, s. 123(3) wisely provides a check on this undesirable development by providing that an appeal to any of these factors made in furtherance of the candidature of any candidate as therein prescribed would constitute a corrupt practice and would render the election of the said candidate void.

In considering the question as to whether the distribution of the impugned poster by the appellant constitutes corrupt practice under s. 123(3), there is one point which has to be borne in mind. The appellant had been adopted as its candidate by the Akali Dal Party. This Party is recognised as a political party by the Election Commission notwithstanding the fact that all of its members are only Sikhs. It is well-known that there are several parties in this country which subscribe to different political and economic ideologies, but the membership of them is either confined to, or predominantly held by, members of particular communities or religions. So long as law does not prohibit the formation of such parties and in fact recognises them for the purpose of election and parliamentary life, it would be necessary to remember that an appeal made by candidates of such parties for votes may, if successful, lead to their election and in an indirect way, may conceivably be influenced by considerations of religion, race, caste, community or language. This infirmity cannot perhaps be avoided so long as parties are allowed to function and are recognised, though their composition may be predominantly based on membership of particular communities or religion. That is why we think, in considering the question as to whether a particular appeal made by a candidate falls within the mischief of s. 123(3), courts should not be astute to read into the words used in the appeal anything more than can be attributed to them on its fair and reasonable construction.

That takes us to the question of construing the impugned poster. The principles which have to be applied in construing such a document are well settled. The document must be read as a whole and its purport and effect determined in a fair, objective and reasonable manner. In reading such documents, it would be unrealistic to ignore the fact that when election meetings are held and appeals are made by candidates of opposing political parties, the atmosphere is usually surcharged with partisan feelings and emotions and the use of hyperboles or exaggerated language, or the adoption of metaphors, and the extravagance of expression in attacking one another, are all a part of the game, and so, when the question about the effect of speeches delivered or pamphlets distributed at election meetings is argued in the cold atmosphere of a judicial chamber, some allowance must be made and the impugned speeches or pamphlets must be construed in that light. In doing so, however, it would be unreasonable to ignore the question as to what the effect of the said speech or pamphlet would be on the mind of the ordinary voter who attends such meetings and reads the pamphlets or hears the speeches. It is in the light of these well-established principles that we must now turn to the impugned pamphlet. (at pp 793–5) (of SCR): (at pp 143–4 of AIR)

42. The test applied in the decision was to construe the meaning of the word 'Panth' not in the abstract but in the context of its use. The conclusion reached was that the word 'Panth' used in the poster did not mean Sikh religion and, therefore, the appeal to the voters was not to vote for the candidate because of his religion. Referring to an earlier decision in *Jagdev Singh Sidhanti v. Pratap Singh Daulta & Others*, 1964 (6) SCR 750, it was reiterated as under:

...Political issues which form the subject-matter of controversies at election meetings may indirectly and incidentally introduce considerations of language or religion, but in deciding the question as to whether corrupt practice has been committed under s.123(3), care must be taken to consider the impugned speech or appeal carefully and always in the light of the relevant political controversy... (at page 799) (of SCR): (at p. 146 para 17 of AIR).

43. Thus, it cannot be doubted, particularly in view of the Constitution Bench decisions of this Court that the words 'Hinduism' or 'Hindutva' are not necessarily to be understood and construed narrowly, confined only to the strict Hindu religious practices unrelated to the culture and ethos of the people of India, depicting the way of life of the Indian people. Unless the context of a speech indicates a contrary meaning or use, in the abstract these terms are indicative more of a way of life of the Indian people and are not confined merely to describe persons practising the Hindu religion as a faith.

44. Considering the terms 'Hinduism' or 'Hindutva' *per se* as depicting hostility, enmity or intolerance towards other religious faiths or professing communalism, proceeds form an improper appreciation and perception of the true meaning of these expressions

emerging from the detailed discussion in earlier authorities of this Court. Misuse of these expressions to promote communalism cannot alter the true meaning of these terms. The mischief resulting from the misuse of the terms by anyone in his speech has to be checked and not its permissible use. It is indeed very unfortunate, if in spite of the liberal and tolerant features of 'Hinduism' recognised in judicial decisions, these terms are misused by anyone during the elections to gain any unfair political advantage. Fundamentalism of any colour or kind must be curbed with a heavy hand to preserve and promote the secular creed of the nation. Any misuse of these terms must, therefore, be dealt with strictly.

45. It is, therefore, a fallacy and an error of law to proceed on the assumption that any reference to Hindutva or Hinduism in a speech makes it automatically a speech based on the Hindu religion as opposed to the other religions or that the use of words 'Hindutva' or 'Hinduism' per se depict an attitude hostile to all persons practising any religion other than the Hindu religion. It is the kind of use made of these words and the meaning sought to be conveyed in the speech with has to be seen and unless such a construction leads to the conclusion that these words were used to appeal for votes for a Hindu candidate on the ground that he is a Hindu or not to vote for a candidate because he is not a Hindu, the mere fact that these words are used in the speech would not bring it within the prohibition of sub-section (3) or (3A) of Section 123. It may well be, that these words are used in a speech to promote secularism or to emphasize the way of life of the Indian people and the Indian culture or ethos, or to criticize the policy of any political party as discriminatory or intolerant. The parliamentary debates, including the clarifications made by the Law Minister quoted earlier, also bring out this difference between the prohibited and permissible speech in this context. Whether a particular speech in which reference is made to Hindutva and/or Hinduism falls within the prohibition under sub-section (3) or (3A) of Section 123 is, therefore, a question of fact in each case.

46. This is the correct premise in our view on which all such matters are to be examined. The fallacy is in the assumption that a speech in which reference is made to Hindutva or Hinduism must be a speech on the ground of Hindu religion so that if the candidate for whom

the speech is made happens to be a Hindu, it must necessarily amount to a corrupt practice under sub-section (3) and/or sub-section (3A) of Section 123 of the R.P. Act. As indicated, there is no such presumption permissible in law contrary to the several Constitution Bench decisions referred herein.

NON-COMPLIANCE OF SECTION 99 OF THE R.P. ACT

47. The contention that the notice given to Bal Thackeray under Section 99 of the R.P. Act was not in conformity with that provision and that there is non-compliance of the requirements of Section 99, has no merit. The notice was given after the entire evidence had been recorded and the learned trial Judge formed the prima facie opinion that the corrupt practices alleged to have been committed under sub-sections (3) and (3A) of Section 123 appeared to have been proved and Bal Thackeray was likely to be named along with the returned candidate to be guilty of those corrupt practices. The notice given was accompanied by copies of pleadings and the entire evidence adduced at the trial for proving those corrupt practices. The notice clearly stated that the noticee had the opportunity to cross-examine such witnesses as had already been examined and of calling evidence in his defence and of being heard. The noticee raised objection to the notice alleging that it was vague, which was rejected by the High Court. That order was challenged by a special leave petition in this Court which was dismissed granting liberty to the notice to apply in the High Court for the precise particulars claimed by him. Ultimately certain portions from the material on record were indicated by the petitioner on such a direction being given by the High Court. In view of the direction of this Court in the special leave petition, it would have been more appropriate for the High Court to indicate the precise portions. However, there is no prejudice caused inasmuch as the portions were indicated by the election petitioner on the High Court's direction. The election petitioner Prabhakar Kashinath Kunte (PW-1) was called for cross-examination on behalf of the noticee. The noticee was given full opportunity to cross-examine the witnesses already examined and to adduce evidence in his defence and to argue his case in the High Court. The noticee Bal Thackeray did not choose to enter the witness box

and, therefore, the material present has to be examined without any denial by the notice as a witness in the case.

48. There is no dispute that no material which was not given to the noticee Bal Thackeray was used against him. We have already indicated that the finding of proof of the corrupt practices alleged in the election petition is based on the three speeches of Bal Thackeray which are not denied either by Dr Ramesh Prabhoo or by Bal Thackeray. Copy of the text of those speeches is also undisputed. All this was furnished to the noticee Bal Thackeray. It is difficult to visualize what prejudice could be caused to the noticee on these facts and how there could be any non-compliance of Section 99 of the R.P. Act in this situation.

49. In order to examine the contention of non-compliance of Section 99, it is necessary to examine the requirements of that provision. Section 99 reads as under:

'99. Other orders to be made by the High Court.

(1) At the time of making an order under section 98 the High Court shall also make an order—

> (a) where any charge is made in the petition of any corrupt practice having been committed at the election, recording—

> > (i) a finding whether any corrupt practice has or has not been proved to have been committed at the election, and the nature of that corrupt practice; and
> > (ii) the names of all persons, if any, who have been proved at the trial to have been guilty of any corrupt practice and the nature of that practice; and

> (b) fixing the total amount of costs payable and specifying the persons by and to whom costs shall be paid:

Provided that a person who is not a party to the petition shall not be named in the order under sub-clause (ii) of clause (a) unless—

> (a) he has been given notice to appear before the High Court and to show cause why he should not be so named; and

(b) if he appears in pursuance of the notice, he has been given an opportunity of cross-examining any witness who has already been examined by the High Court and has given evidence against him, of calling evidence in his defence and of being heard.

(2) In this section and in section 100, the expression "agent" has the same meaning as in section 123.'

50. Sub-section (1) requires that at the time of making an order under Section 98, the High Court shall also make an order recording the names of all persons, if any, who have been proved at the trial to have been guilty of any corrupt practice and the nature of that practice. In other words, while deciding the election petition at the conclusion of the trial and making an order under Section 98 disposing of the election petition in one of the ways specified therein, the High Court is required to record the names of all persons guilty of any corrupt practice which has been proved at the trial. Proviso to sub-section (1) then prescribes that a person who is not a party to the petition shall not be so named unless the condition specified in the proviso is fulfilled. The requirement of the proviso is only in respect of a person who is not a party to the petition and is to be named so that he too has the same opportunity which was available to a party to the petition. The requirement specified is of a notice to appear and show cause why he should not be named and if he appears in pursuance of the notice, he has to be given an opportunity of cross-examining any witness who has already been examined by the High Court and has given evidence against him and also the opportunity of calling evidence in his defence and of being heard. In short, the opportunity which a party to the petition had at the trial to defend against the allegation of corrupt practice is to be given by such a notice to that person of defending himself if he was not already a party to the petition. In other words, the notice has to be equated with a party to the petition for this purpose and is to be given the same opportunity which he would get if he was made a party to the petition.

51. This is the pragmatic test to be applied for deciding the question of compliance of Section 99 of the R.P. Act. If the noticee had the opportunity which he would have got as a party to the petition, then

there can be no case of non-compliance of Section 99. The opportunity required to be given by the proviso to sub-section (1) of Section 99 is the same and not more than that available to a party to the petition to defend himself against the charge of corrupt practice. Applying the above test, there can be no doubt that there is no non-compliance of Section 99 in the present case. The noticee Bal Thackeray had the same opportunity which the returned candidate Dr Ramesh Yeshwant Prabhoo got as a respondent to the petition. The noticee was given the opportunity to cross-examine any witness who had already been examined by the High Court and the witnesses who were considered to have given evidence against him, were also enumerated in the notice; and he was given an opportunity to call evidence in his defence and to be heard.

52. In this situation, the grievance made that specific portions of the material which formed the record at the trial was not precisely indicated to the notice has no merit. It was clear from the pleading that the allegation against the notice was in respect of the three speeches made by him, the particulars of which were given and the text of those speeches also was available to the noticee which he did not even deny. On these facts, there is no ground to allege non-compliance of Section 99 of the R.P. Act. This contention on behalf of the noticee Bal Thackeray is, therefore, rejected and the objection raised in the appeal of Bal Thackeray of non-compliance of Section 99 of the R.P. Act has no merit.

53. We would now proceed to examine the facts of this case.

SPEECHES

54. It is in the light of the above discussion and the meaning of sub-sections (3) and (3A) of Section 123 that the effect of the alleged offending speeches has to be examined. The three speeches which were made on 29.11.1987, 9.12.1987 and 10.12.1987 amount to corrupt practices under sub-sections (3) and (3A) of Section 123, while the speech of 9.12.1987 is a corrupt practice only under sub-section (3) thereof. The returned candidate Dr Ramesh Yeshwant Prabhoo was present in all the three meetings in which these speeches were given by Bal Thackeray. The consent of Dr Prabhoo for these speeches is

implied from his conduct including his personal presence in all the three meetings.

55. Certain extracts from the alleged speeches of Bal Thackeray, translated in English, are expressly pleaded in the election petition, as under:

From Speech of 29.11.1987

'We are fighting this election for the protection of Hinduism. Therefore, we do not care for the votes of the Muslims. This country belongs to Hindus and will remain so.'

From Speech of 9.12.1987

'Hinduism will triumph in this election and we must become hon'ble recipients of this victory to ward off the danger on Hinduism, elect Ramesh Prabhoo to join with Chhagan Bhujbal who is already there. You will find Hindu temples underneath if all the mosques are dug out. Anybody who stands against the Hindus should be showered or worshipped with shoes. A candidate by name Prabhoo should be led to victory in the name of religion.'

From Speech of 10.12.1987

'We have gone with the ideology of Hinduism. Shiv Sena will implement this ideology. Though this country belongs to Hindus, Ram and Krishna are insulted. (They) valued the Muslim votes more than your votes: we do not want the Muslim votes. A snake like Shahabuddin is sitting in the Janata Party, a man like Nihal Ahmed is also in Janata Party. So the residents of Vile Parle should bury this party (Janata Party).'

56. It has been pleaded in the election petition that the above utterances in the three meetings are examples to show that the appeal to voters emphasized that Dr Ramesh Prabhoo was the only person who could represent the Hindu community and, therefore, the voters should vote for Ramesh Prabhoo in the name of religion. The full text of the speeches was adduced in evidence and the contents thereof are not disputed. It may be mentioned that a notice under Section 99 of

the R.P. Act was issued to Bal Thackeray who merely filed an affidavit but did not enter the witness box. The true import and impact of these speeches has, therefore, to be adjudged in the light of the evidence including the statement of Dr Ramesh Yeshwant Prabhoo without the version in evidence of Bal Thackeray.

57. The case was argued even before us on a demurrer treating the contents of the speeches as reproduced in the full text in evidence, of which the specific portions pleaded in the election petition are extracts. The question is: Whether these speeches amount to corrupt practices under sub-section (3) and/or (3A) of Section 123 as held by the High Court?

58. We may now quote certain extracts from the three speeches of Bal Thackeray on which reliance has been placed in particular by Shri Ashok Desai to support the judgment of the High Court that they constitute the said corrupt practices. These are:

First speech on 29.11.1987

'All my Hindu brothers, sisters and mothers gathered here. ...Today Dr Prabhoo has been put up as candidate from your Parle. ...But here one cannot do anything at anytime about the snake in the form of Khalistan and Muslim. ...The entire country has been ruined and therefore we took the stand of Hindutva and by taking the said stand we will step in the Legislative Assembly. ...Unless we step forward strongly it would be difficult for us to live because there would be war of religion. ...Muslims will come, What will you Hindu (people) do. Are you going to throw 'Bhasma' (i.e. ashes) on them. ...We won't mind if we do not get a vote from a single Muslim and we are not at all desirous to win an election with such votes. ...therefore, there is a dire need of the voice of Hindutva and therefore please send Shiv Sena to Legislative Assembly. ...Who are (these) Muslims? Who are these *lande*? Once Vasant Dada had called me when he was a Chief Minister. He told me that rest is O.K. But asked me as to why I was calling them lande. But is it correct if they call us *Kafer* (i.e. traitor) then we will certainly call them lande ...They should bear in

mind that this country is of Hindus, the same shall remain
of Hindus. ...if Shiv Sena comes to power and if the
morchas come—first of all (we) shall make them come.
Everybody will have to take 'diksha' (i.e. initiation) of
Hindu religion...'

Second speech of 9.12.1987

'...The victory will not be mine or of Dr Prabhoo or of
Shiv Sena but the victory will be that of Hinduism. You
will be instrumental in victory and you should become an
instrument for the same. At last you have the right to get
rid of the difficulties faced by your caste, creed, gods,
deities and Hindu religion. ...Therefore, I want to say that
today we are standing for Hinduism. ...Whatever Masjids
are there, if one starts digging the same, one will find
Hindu temples under the same. ...If anybody stands
against Hindustan you should show courage by performing pooja (i.e. worship) with shoes. ...And a person by
name Prabhoo who is contesting the election in the name
of religion surge ahead (in the assembly). A 'Jawan'—like
Prabhoo should go there (in the assembly)...'

Third speech of 10.12.1987

'...It will do, if we do not get a vote from any Muslim.
If anybody from them is present at this place he should
think for himself. I am not in need of their votes. But I
want your vote. ...You must send only Dr Ramesh
Prabhoo of Shiv Sena, otherwise Hindus will be finished.
It will not take much for Hindustan to be green (i.e.
Pakistan?).'

59. As earlier stated, the three speeches of Bal Thackeray from
which the above extracts have been quoted are admitted. Similarly the
interview of Dr Ramesh Yeshwant Prabhoo and its text published in
Janmabhoomi Prawasi is admitted. Dr Prabhoo was the Mayor of
Bombay. Dr Prabhoo (RW-1) admitted his presence in the meetings
held on 29.11.1987, 9.12.1987 and 10.12.1987 in which the above
speeches were given by Bal Thackeray. He admitted speaking himself

also in these meetings. He has said nothing in his statement to suggest that he did not consent to the contents of the speeches of Bal Thackeray. In his deposition, he has expressly admitted that the speeches of Bal Thackeray were according to his election campaign. The element of the candidate's consent for the appeal to the voters made by Bal Thackeray in his speeches is, therefore, adequately proved. About his interview published in the *Janmabhoomi Prawasi*, issue of 9.12.1987, he said that the report is substantially correct, even though the first paragraph of that news item is incorrect. Omitting the first paragraph of the news item which he denied, certain portions, translated into English, from the remaining news item publishing the interview are as under:

> '...Dr Prabhoo told me that there was a Hindu wave in Parle. The battle is between Hindus and Muslims i.e. to say between nationalist and anti-nationalist... Supremely confident about his victory in the Vile Parle bye-election, Dr Prabhoo discounted any possibility of his defeats but he added that if he loses, it will mean that Hinduism has lost,...'

60. The appeal made to the voters by Bal Thackeray in his aforesaid speech was a clear appeal to the Hindu voters to vote for Dr Ramesh Prabhoo because he is a Hindu. The clear import of the above extracts in each of the three speeches is to this effect. The first speech also makes derogatory reference to Muslims by calling them 'snake' and referring to them as *lande* (derogatory term used for those practising circumcision). The language used in the context, amounted to an attempt to promote feelings of enmity or hatred between Hindus and Muslims on the ground of religion. The first speech, therefore, also constitutes a corrupt practice under sub-section (3A).

61. The High Court has held the second speech to fall only under sub-section (3) and not sub-section (3A), but the third speech has been held to fall both under sub-section (3) and (3A). We have already held the third speech also to constitute the corrupt practice under sub-section (3). The correctness of the English translation of a part of the third speech was found to be defective at the hearing and, therefore, an agreed fresh translation thereof was taken on record. Reading the

speech in the light of the fresh agreed translation of the defective portion, it appears to us that the High Court's finding that the third speech also amounts to the corrupt practice under sub-section (3A) cannot be affirmed, even though this variation is of no consequence to the ultimate result.

62. Our conclusion is that all the three speeches of Bal Thackeray amount to corrupt practice under sub-section (3),while the first speech is a corrupt practice also under sub-section (3A) of Section 123 of the R.P. Act. Since the appeal made to the voters in these speeches was to vote for Dr Ramesh Prabhoo on the ground of his religion as a Hindu and the appeal was made with the consent of the candidate Dr Ramesh Prabhoo, he is guilty of these corrupt practices. For the same reason, Bal Thackeray is also guilty of these corrupt practices and, therefore, liable to be named in accordance with Section 99 of the R.P. Act of which due compliance has been made in the present case.

63. We cannot help recording our distress at this kind of speeches given by a top leader of a political party. The lack of restraint in the language used and the derogatory terms used therein to refer to a group of people in an election speech is indeed to be condemned. The likely impact of such language used by a political leader is greater. It is, therefore, a greater need for the leaders to be more circumspect and careful in the kind of language they use in election campaigns. This is essential not only for maintaining decency and propriety in the election campaign but also for the preservation of the proper and time honoured values forming part of our cultural heritage and for a free and fair poll in a secular democracy. The offending speeches in the present case discarded the cherished values of our rich cultural heritage and tended to erode the secular polity. We say this, with the fervent hope that our observation has some chastening effect in future election campaigns.

64. For the aforesaid reasons, both the appeals must fail. We may observe that considerable irrelevant material was brought on record during the trial at the instance of both the parties which, apart from needlessly enlarging the scope of the trial, has led to needless extra expense and wastage of time even in the hearing of these appeals. In these circumstances, it is appropriate to direct the parties to bear their own costs in this Court. Accordingly, both the appeals are dismissed.

Bibliography

Agarwal, Purushottam, 'Savarkar, Surat and Draupadi', in Tanika Sarkar and Urvashi Butalia (eds), *Women and the Hindu Right* (New Delhi: Kali for Women, 1995).

Agnes, Flavia, 'Two Riots and After: A Fact-finding Report on Bandar (East)', *EPW* (February 13, 1993).

Basu, Tapan *et. al.*, *Khaki Shorts, Saffron Flags: A Critique of the Hindu Right* (Delhi: Orient Longman, 1993).

Baxi Upendra, 'The Struggle for the Redefinition of Secularism in India: Some Preliminary Reflections', in Rudolf C. Heredia and Edward Mathias (eds), *Secularism and Liberation* (1995).

Berger, Peter, *The Social Reality of Religion* (London: Allen Lane, 1973).

Bhargava, Rajeev (ed.), *Secularism and its Critics* (New Delhi: Oxford University Press, 1998).

————— 'Giving Secularism its Due', *EPW* (July 9, 1994).

————— 'What is Secularism for?' in Bhargava (ed.), *Secularism and its Critics* (1998).

Bharucha, Rustom, 'In the Name of the Secular: Cultural Interactions and Interventions', *EPW* (November 5, 1994).

Bilgrami, Akeel, 'Two Concepts of Secularism: Reason, Modernity and Archimedean Ideal', *EPW* (July 4, 1994).

Chandra, Bipan, *Communalism in Modern India* (Delhi: Vani Educational Books, Vikas, 1984).

Chatterjee, Partha, 'Secularism and Toleration', *EPW* (July 9, 1994).

Chaudhari, R. L., *The Concept of Secularism in Indian Constitution* (1987).

Deoras, Balasaheb, *Answers Questions* (Bangalore: Sahitya Sindhu, 1984).

Deshmukh, Nana, *RSS: Victim of Slander* (New Delhi: Vision Books, 1979).

Engineer, Asgar Ali, 'Bombay Shames India', *EPW* (January 16, 1993).

————— 'Secularism in India: Theory and Practice', in *Secularism and Liberation*, (1995).

Feldman, Stephen M., 'Principle, History and Power: The Limits of First Amendment Religion Clauses', *Iowa Law Review* (1996).

Gajendragadkar, P. B., 'Secularism: Its Implications for Law and Life in India' in G. S. Sharma (ed.), *Secularism: Its Implications for Law and Life in India* (Bombay: N. M. Tripathi, 1966).

Galanter, Marc, 'Hinduism, Secularism and the Indian Judiciary' in Bhargava (ed.), *Secularism and its Critics* (New Delhi: Oxford University Press, 1998).

Gowalkar, M. S., *We or Our Nationhood Defined* (Nagpur: Bharat Publications, 1939).

————— *Bunch of Thoughts* (Bangalore: Vikrama Prakashan, 1966).

————— 'From Red Fort Grounds' (November 14, 1965) (Transcript, New Delhi: Nehru Memorial Museum and Library).

Hall, Stuart, 'Cultural Identity and Cinematic Representation' in Houston Baker Jr. et. al. (eds), *Black British Cultural Studies: A Reader* (Chicago: University of Chicago Press, 1996).

Heredia, Rudolf C. and Edward Mathias (eds), *Secularism and Liberation: Perspectives and Strategies for India Today* (New Delhi: Indian Social Institute, 1995).

Jayaprasad, K., *RSS and Hindu Nationalism* (New Delhi: Deep and Deep, 1991).

Kapur, Ratna and Brenda Cossman, 'Communalising Gender/Engendering Community: Women, Legal Discourse and the Saffron Agenda, *EPW* (May, 1993).

———— *Subversive Sites: Feminist Engagement with Law in India* (New Delhi: Sage, 1996).

———— 'On Women, Equality and the Constitution: Through the Looking Glass of Feminism', *National Law School Journal*, Special Edition: Feminism and Law, (1993).

Kapur, Ratna, 'Who Draws the line? Feminist Reflections on Speech and Censorship', *EPW* (April 20, 1996).

———— 'A Love Song to our Mongrel Selves: Hybridity, Sexuality and the Law', *Social and Legal Studies* (forthcoming, 1999).

Luthra, V. P., *The Concept of Secular State and India* (Calcutta: Oxford University Press, 1964).

Madan, T. N., 'Secularism in its Place', *Journal of Asian Studies* 46:4 (November 1987).

———— 'Whither Indian Secularism?' *Modern Asian Studies* 27:3 (1993).

Minow, Martha, 'Supreme Court, 1986 Term, Foreword: Justice Engendered', *Harvard Law Review* 10 (1987).

———— *Making All the Difference: Inclusion, Exclusion and American Law* (Ithaca, NY: Cornell University Press, 1990).

———— 'Putting Up and Putting Down: Tolerance Reconsidered, *Osgoode Hall Law Journal* 28 (1990).

Nauriya, Anil, 'The Hindutva Judgments: A Warning Signal', *EPW* (January 10, 1996).

Nandy, Ashis, 'The Politics of Secularism and the Recovery of Religious Tolerance' in Rajeev Bhargava (ed.), *Secularism and its Critics* (New Delhi: Oxford University Press, 1998).

———— 'An Anti-Secularist Manifesto', Seminar (October, 1985).

Pantham, Thomas, 'Indian Secularism and its Critics: Some Reflections', *The Review of Politics* 59:3 (1997).

Qaiser, Rizwan, 'The Conceptualization of Communalism and Hindu Rashtra', in Rudolf C. Heredia and Edward Mathias (eds), *Secularism and Liberation* (1995).

Report of the Sri Krishna Commission, August 6, 1998.

Roy, Arundhati, 'The End of Imagination', *Outlook* (August 3, 1998).

Rushdie, Salman, *The Moor's Last Sigh*, (1995).

Sarkar, Tanika and Urvashi Butalia (eds), *Women and the Hindu Right* (New Delhi: Kali for Women, 1995).

Savarkar, V. D., *Hindutva: Who is a Hindu?* (1929) 4e (Pune: S. P. Gokhale, 1949).

Scanlon, T. M., 'The Difficulty of Tolerance' in Rajeev Bhargava (ed.), *Secularism and its Critics* (1998).

Seshadri, H. V., *The Way* (New Delhi: Suruchi Prakashan, 1991).

Sen, Amartya, 'The Threats to Secular India', *The New York Times Review of Books* XL-7 (April 8, 1993).

———— 'Secularism and its Discontents' in Rajeev Bhargava (ed.), *Secularism and its Critics* (New Delhi: Oxford University Press, 1998).

Sharma, G. S. (ed.), *Secularism: Its Implications for Law and Life in India* (Bombay: N. M. Tripathi, 1966).

Shelat, J. M., *Secularism: Principles and Applications* (1972).

Smith, Donald Eugene, *India as a Secular State* (Princeton University Press, 1964).

Tripathi, P. K., 'Secularism, Law and Constitution of India' in V. K. Sinha (ed.), *Secularism in India* (Bombay: Lalvani Publication House, 1966).

———— 'Secularism: Law and the Constitutional Provision and Judicial Review' in Sharma (ed.), *Secularism: Its Implications for Law and Life in India* (1966).

Upadhyaya, Prakash Chandra, 'The Politics of Indian Secularism', *Modern Asian Studies* (1992).

Upadhyaya, Deendayal, *Integral Humanism*, (1965).